D1713504

The Children's Mahabharata

Shanta Rameshwar Rao

Orient Longman

ORIENT LONGMAN LIMITED

Regd. Office
3-6-272 Himayatnagar, Hyderabad 500 029

Other Offices
Kamani Marg, Ballard Estate, Bombay 400 038
17 Chittaranjan Avenue, Calcutta 700 072
160 Anna Salai, Madras 600 002
1/24 Asaf Ali Road, New Delhi 110 002
80/1 Mahatma Gandhi Road, Bangalore 560 001
365 Shaheed Nagar, Bhubaneshwar 751 007
41/316 'Gour Mohan', Ambady Lane, Chittoor Road, Cochin 682 011
S.C. Goswami Road, Panbazar, Guwahati 781 001
3-6-272 Himayatnagar, Hyderabad 500 029
28/31, 15 Ashok Marg, Lucknow 226 001
City Centre Ashok, Govind Mitra Road, Patna 800 004

Reprinted 1973, 1980, 1986, 1989, 1991, 1995

ISBN 81 250 0905 1

Cover designed by
Suvarchala Bhale Rao

Published by Orient Longman Ltd.
R. Kamani Marg, Ballard Estate, Bombay 400 038
and Printed by in India at S.G. Printers,
Lower Parel, Bombay 400 011

FOREWORD

The Mahabharata is one of the eternal epics of the world. As long as human beings remain what they are and are moved by passions and feelings, as long as the struggle between good and evil continues to rage in the human heart, as long as mankind is faced with the problems of war and peace, the Mahabharata will continue to remain a source of aesthetic enjoyment and moral and intellectual enlightenment.

There used to be a time not more than three or four decades back when children listened to the tales from the Mahabharata from their mothers or grandmothers. But times have changed now and cheap stories of 'adventure' and crime and 'funnies' from the 'developed' societies are fast becoming the main fare for the minds of our growing children. It is, therefore, a matter of real satisfaction that the everlasting lore of Mahabharata should be presented in a simple and interesting style in these pages by Rani Shanta Rameshwar Rao. The author deserves the gratitude of the present generation.

It is not, however, enough that a book like this should be printed and published. It should be the responsibility of parents, especially mothers, to place this volume in the hands of their growing children and kindle in them sufficient interest so that it might claim their attention.

New Delhi
Feb. 16, 1968

JAYAPRAKASH NARAYAN

I would like to thank:

Shri Jayaprakash Narayan for going through the book and writing the foreword.

Dr. B. M. Lott of the British Council, Director of Studies, C. I. E., Hyderabad, for his help and encouragement in its writing.

Mrs. Agnes Alex for typing it out.

SHANTA RAMESHWAR RAO

To
MY MOTHER

INTRODUCTION

THE MAHABHARATA tells
the story of the warrior
princes, who were called the
Kauravas and the Pandavas,
and who lived in India many
centuries ago. It tells of their
rivalries and their adventures,
and of the great war which
they fought on the field of
Kurukshetra.

They were cousins—sons of
brothers, and they belonged to

the clan or family of the Kurus. The Aryans who made their homes in the plains of Northern India lived in family groups called clans. The Kurus were princes and warriors, trained from childhood to warlike pursuits. They lived and ruled in India, and had their empire over much of the land covered today by Uttar Pradesh and Delhi.

If you are an Indian child it is very unlikely that you have not heard of the Mahabharata. For, over the centuries this epic and the characters and situations described in it have become part of our very being. If you are a boy and have four brothers or four friends in whose company you are constantly seen, it is almost certain that at one time or another some one has laughingly referred to you as the Pancha Pandavas. If you grow up to be a tall, well built, brawny type, some one might quite possibly have nicknamed you a "Bhima". If you are a girl and have not braided up your hair but have allowed it to remain loose down your back, you might have had your grandmother or an elderly aunt point out to you and say: "Here comes our Draupadi!" and perhaps she would explain to you that when Draupadi had been dragged by the hair to the assembly hall of the Kauravas her tresses had come loose. Then she had vowed that she would neither comb her hair nor bind it up until Bhima had killed Dushahsana and avenged the dishonour done to her.

The Mahabharata is known through the length and breadth of our country. From out of it come innumerable references—proverbs and sayings and wise and amusing little stories or anecdotes which, though constantly repeated, never lose their beauty or charm. In almost every remote nook and corner of India the Mahabharata appears and curiously enough the characters take on the ways and manners of that particular region. If you came from a village in the Madras State you would think that the entire action of the epic took place in the area surrounding your village, among people who lived and spoke and worked and played as you and your neighbours did. On the other hand, to a child from Bengal the characters of the Mahabharata would be Bengali, speaking the Bengali language and following Bengali customs. What is even more interesting is that the Mahabharata has travelled (along with other ancient Indian literature) over the sea to countries as far as Indonesia, Siam and Cambodia. In these lands the people tell the story, and the characters live and move and belong as if they had sprung out of the native soil. Thus the different versions of the epic differ—it would be strange indeed if they did not. For stories told by word of mouth (as our epics were for long, and still continue to a great extent to be) will naturally change in the telling—a little here and a little there—an addition made here by one teller with a vivid imagination, an omission made there by another with a bad memory—and over a period of time broad changes take place. But the basic story remains the same.

No one is quite certain about the date the Mahabharata was first written, but scholars say that it is one of the oldest literary works known to man. It is also the world's longest literary work. As we know the epic today, it contains a 100,000 stanzas and is eight times longer than Homer's Iliad and Odyssey put together.

In India people call the Mahabharata the fifth Veda, for in it may be found every branch of knowledge. The poets who composed it—(for it does not seem possible that this vast poem could be the work of one single individual)—have woven into it history and legend, myth and folklore, fable and parable, philosophy and religion, statecraft and the art of war, morals and romance. It is like a wonderfully rich fabric of innumerable patterns and colours. In the Mahabharata story you see reflected as in a mirror the lives of the Indian people. Princes and kings move in stately procession upon the Mahabharata stage in the company of proud warriors and men of rich and noble ancestry: and side by side with them walk the common folk. We see in it the history of the Aryan settlement and advance, their contact with their dark-skinned neighbours—who ruled the country before they came,—their rivalries and adventures and wars and their entire way of life.

In the following pages is the barest story of the mighty epic. It is like one strand out of the whole rich fabric and yet in it I have tried to recapture a little of its grandeur, its beauty and its colour. For a brief minute as you read the book it may be that the characters will flash past you: the gentle-hearted Yudhishthira ruling over his newly built empire as a wise and kind father rules over his homestead, a prince who hated war and violence and yet was drawn into it in spite of or perhaps because of his very goodness; Arjuna, the warrior, fearless and skilful and yet tormented always by doubts; Abhimanyu, young, daring and impulsive, who knew not what fear was; Draupadi, the dark princess in whose heart burned a great anger which she would not allow to be extinguished,—an anger that consumed all things at last in its fearful flames, —so that only bitter memories remained in the end like ashes after a mighty fire.

The story begins with a blind man sitting upon the throne. Dhritarashtra is blind, says the poet. But this is his way of telling us that the old king was like hundreds of men who have not the light and the vision of intelligence. He sat on a throne, and ruled over men, but the throne was too big for him and he was not worthy of it. For he was a weak and stupid and cunning little man. Men obeyed his commands because he was king, though they knew him to be stupid and weak, and in his folly and his blindness he caused the destruction of the empire and the race. Gandhari, his wife, is different: she is wise and great and intelligent. She understands: and yet, such is her devotion to her husband that she blind-folds her eyes to share his infirmity and refuses to see. How often do we not see in the history of countries men like Dhritarashtra in power, men of poor intelligence and small, narrow minds, who lead their people and their countries to ruin, because of their blindness and stupidity! As for Duryodhana he destroyed himself because of his over-riding jealousy. Duryodhana's heart was so clouded over with anger and envy that he knew no happiness though he had everything in the world to make him happy.

Very different from Duryodhana is his loyal friend Karna. Karna is noble and upright and will not stoop to anything low and unchivalrous. He is a man of truth and principle, of great charity and noble conduct. Fortune frowned on Karna from the day of his birth, and all his life it was as if he was swimming against mighty currents or battling formidable enemies who surrounded him on all sides. But he was nothing if he was not a man of action and he fought endlessly, never heeding the consequences: he fought bravely and nobly, and nearly always he fought in the face of certain defeat. To many people it is Karna who is the central figure and hero of the epic.

Such then are the characters of the Mahabharata: men and women not unlike men and women in other centuries and other lands—people who lived and loved and hated, who grieved and were happy, who were compassionate and revengeful, who were tormented by jealousies or eaten up by pride—deceitful, cunning, charitable, chivalrous. It is the story of heroic men and brave women who were inspiring and noble even in tragedy.

The Mahabharata is a book for all times and all occasions and there is no human situation, it seems, that it does not mention or treat of. Its message is for all people, young and old, men, women and children. No two people would perhaps read in it the same meaning. For each individual who reads or hears it the Mahabharata brings a different message according to the way in which he looks for it. And this in the end is perhaps the secret of its power and its popularity.

CONTENTS

CHAPTER		PAGE
I	Devavrata	1
II	The Unhappy Princess	21
III	The Coming of Karna	33
IV	The Pandava Princes	40
V	Drona	45
VI	A Wicked Plot	58
VII	Ekalavya	64
VIII	Karna Faces Arjuna	74
IX	Karna and the Brahmastra Weapon	87
X	Duryodhana Plots Again	97
XI	The Pandavas Escape	103
XII	A Silent City and a Demon King	111
XIII	The Pandavas Win Draupadi	118
XIV	The Pandavas Return to Hastinapura	130
XV	The Pandavas Build Indraprastha and Extend their Empire	135
XVI	The Slaying of Jarasandha	141
XVII	Yudhisthira Performs the Rajasuya Sacrifice	148
XVIII	Shakuni Makes his Appearance	155
XIX	Vidura Goes to Indraprastha	163
XX	The Gambling Match	167

XXI	The Pandavas in Exile	187
XXII	The Pandavas Come to Matsya, and Kichaka Meets his Death	204
XXIII	Duryodhana's Attack on Matsya	216
XXIV	Prince Uttara Kumar Goes into Battle	223
XXV	The Pandavas Make themselves Known	231
XXVI	The Pandavas and their Allies Confer together	238
XXVII	Envoys and Missions	244
XXVIII	Kunti Meets Karna	255
XXIX	Preparations for War	263
XXX	Kurukshetra and After	276

CHAPTER I

DEVAVRATA

ONG ago there ruled over the kingdom of Hastinapura in the ancient land of Bharata a king named Shantanu, head of the great Aryan clan of the Kurus. His subjects loved and honoured him as a worthy ruler. They trusted him completely, for they knew him to be wise and just. When therefore he called their representatives together to tell them of his intention to name his only son, the beloved prince Devavrata, heir to his throne, they were delighted beyond measure. They received his announcement with great joy and praised Shantanu for his foresight and good sense. Preparations were forthwith made for the joyful occasion, and on the chosen day, the young prince was named heir to Hastinapura's throne amid great pomp and ceremony.

The people had reason to be happy, for Devavrata, though young in years, was famed for his goodness and wisdom. He was a tall handsome lad, and his eyes and face seemed to glow with a hidden light. Men said that that was because his mother had been no ordinary mortal: Devavrata was the son of the river Goddess Ganga. It was also said that Devavrata himself had been an immortal—Prabhasa—whom an angry Rishi[1] had cursed for a sin he had committed. For his sin Prabhasa had been doomed to spend a life-time on the earth as a mortal.

It had happened in this way:

Prabhasa was the youngest of the seven Vasu brothers. The Vasus were gods and had everything they could desire to make them happy. But they were not happy; for in their hearts they constantly craved for things they could not get and they were never satisfied. Then one day their greedy and covetous eyes fell on a cow that belonged to the Rishi Vasishtha. She was so beautiful that they wanted her instantly and were tormented by their desire to possess her. They schemed and plotted together trying to find ways and means of getting her and eventually they decided to steal her. However, when the moment came to do so,

[1] Sage; wise man.

the six older brothers suddenly grew afraid, knowing how angry Vasishtha would be when he found out. Prabhasa alone, spurred on by the taunts of his wife, was ready to do the deed. He stole the cow and brought her to his brothers, and together they hid her away. But not for long. For the Rishi, wild with grief at his loss, searched everywhere, until he found the thieves crouching guilty-faced in heaven. He strode up to them, and, as he took possession of his beloved cow, he cursed them in his anger for their sin—for their greed and their covetousness and their deceitfulness. They would fall from their high estate, he said, and be born on the mortal earth as mortal men, for they did not deserve to be gods. Heaven and its joys were not meant for sinful creatures such as they!

His words struck fear and sorrow into the hearts of the Vasus. They had no wish to be born as mortals. Human beings must suffer pain and sorrow and eventually death. It seemed to them that one human lifetime on the earth was too long to spend away from heaven. They fell at his feet and begged forgiveness, and when they did so, the Rishi's heart melted and he relented.

"I cannot take away my curse," he said. "But I can soften it and make it easier for you to bear."

Then he told them that for the six older brothers who had only sinned in thought, desiring the cow and plotting how to get her, their life on earth would be short, the space of only a few hours. But Prabhasa who had done the deed must suffer the consequences. Prabhasa must spend a full lifetime on the earth as a mortal. Prabhasa wept bitterly to hear this, but the Rishi consoled him. He would be a mortal above all other mortals, said Vasishtha, and he would live a life of such wisdom and glory that his name would be known over the earth and in heaven, and all men would honour him!

"Go now," Vasishtha continued in a kinder tone. "Go to the Goddess Ganga and she will help you."

The Vasus did as they were told. They hurried to the river Goddess Ganga to seek her help. They fell at her feet and told her their sad story.

"Help us," they prayed "Help us, O Goddess. Come down to the earth and be our mother, and we shall take birth in your womb. And when we are born, in that same hour, take us away and put an end to our lives so that our time on earth may be soon ended, and we may return to our heavenly home."

The Goddess Ganga took pity on them, and agreed to their suggestion.

That was how it came about that one day in the years of Shantanu's youth, he met, of a sudden, a beautiful woman upon the bank of the river Ganga. So beautiful was she indeed that Shantanu was struck with love for her. He went up to her and, though he did not know her, nor anything about her, he spoke to her and begged her to go with him and be his wife and queen.

She did not seem to think this strange at all. She was willing enough to do as he said, she told him, but only if he agreed to certain conditions that she laid down. She warned him that these conditions would not be easy. But Shantanu was ready to go to any length to get this beautiful girl for a bride. Then the girl spoke to her royal suitor:

"If I am to marry you," she said, "you must promise never to question me—neither about who I am, nor where I come from; and you must promise me too that you will not

5

cross me whatever I do, good or evil! Can you agree to these conditions, O King Shantanu? I warn you, you will not find it easy!" They were strange conditions to make, but Shantanu was so far gone out of his wits with love that he was ready to promise anything. "Anything— anything you say, dear one," he babbled. "I will promise to do whatever you demand."

Then the woman smiled and allowed him to lead her to the palace where they were married, and where they lived happily for a whole year. She proved to be a good and dutiful wife, sweet-natured and gracious, and Shantanu thought himself the happiest man in the world. He seemed to be living in a golden dream. He did not know what lay in store for him. In time, a baby was born to the royal couple—a little son—and Shantanu's cup of happiness seemed now to brim over. But that night a dreadful thing happened. Shantanu woke up to see his wife slipping out of the door with the child in her arms. Surprised he followed her. He saw her walk out of the palace gates and down the street until she came to the river bank. There in the pale moonlight she stood, and then suddenly, to his horror, Shantanu saw her lift the baby and throw him out into the dark,

Shantanu saw her lift the baby and throw him
into the dark swirling waters.

swirling waters. Shantanu was aghast. He opened his mouth to cry out and speak, but he caught the warning look in her eye and he remembered the promise he had made to her— to say nothing to her, never to question her, whatever she did, good or evil. So remembering, he remained silent, though his heart wept. He wondered who and what she was, demon or human, but dared not speak. The terrible deed done, the queen turned calmly and walked to the palace and Shantanu followed her, trembling in every limb, and pale and cold with fear.

But back in the palace, Shantanu found himself wondering if it had all been an evil dream, for his wife became once more the sweet and gentle woman he knew and loved. He had nothing at all to complain about—for she went about her duties so cheerfully and graciously that he could scarcely believe his eyes—until another year went by and the second child was born, and the second child met the same fate as the first had done! For the mother who had borne him carried him away at dead of night and drowned him in the dreadful waters of the river, while the horrified grief-stricken Shantanu looked on in silence, not daring to speak because of his promise.

Then yet another year went by, and a third
boy was born, and he fared no better. The
queen drowned him as she had done the other
two. After him came the fourth, the fifth and the
sixth. Each year Shantanu's wife gave birth to
a son, and each year she killed the baby with
her own hands within a few hours of its birth.
Shantanu was mad with grief and fear. He did
not know that his sons were the Vasus, being
freed from their curse to return to the joys of
heaven.

When the seventh child came, he followed
her again to the river bank as he had done so
many times before. She carried the baby in
her arms and Shantanu felt he could bear it
no longer. He was desperate, and this time he
made up his mind to save the child from death,
come what may. And so when his wife was
about to cast the little one into the river he
rushed forward with drawn sword, crying out
to her to stop, and he held her hand. Then in
a voice choking with grief and anger, he reproached her bitterly: "Who are you?" he cried.
"Are you human or are you an evil demoness
in human guise? Six children born of your
womb you have destroyed and killed in cold
blood—and not once been moved by motherly

instinct, or love or pity. But this seventh one
shall live. This one child at least shall live, for
I have come to save him."

At these words the woman who was his wife
smiled a strange smile.

"You have broken your promise to me, O
Shantanu!" she reminded him softly. "You have
sought to know who I am: you have crossed me
and now I can stay with you no longer."

Shantanu stared at her amazed. Her words
seemed to strike a sudden cold fear in his heart.
"Where?" he cried out, "Where will you go?"
But she only smiled her mysterious smile.

"What will become of me?" he went on and
begged her not to forsake him; for in spite of
all that had happened, he knew he loved her to
distraction, and could not bear the thought of
losing her. "Let us forget what has happened,"
he said, "let us start a new life together."

His tears began to fall and when she saw his
distress, she pitied him and spoke to him gently.
She told him her story—explaining how she
had come down to the earth to free the seven
Vasus from their curse. But now her work was
completed and she must go back to the heavenly
regions where her home was. She must take the
child with her for the present, for he was too young

to be left without a mother. But one day, when he was older, he would come back to Shantanu, for his place was in his father's kingdom where his heritage awaited him.

Shantanu did not know what to think. But as he stood there staring in astonishment, the Goddess Ganga vanished, merging into the waters of the river, and he found himself alone on the riverside. Slowly, sadly, he retraced his steps and returned to the palace.

*   *   *   *   *

Seven years went by and then one day the Goddess Ganga returned. Shantanu was walking on the river bank one evening, when a fearful storm arose. The sky grew dark and the winds howled and screeched around him. Shantanu was about to hurry away to take shelter, when he saw a child. He was a little boy, a little naked boy, and he sat on the river bank all alone, laughing. He had a toy bow in his hand and a quiver of little golden arrows and he shot them into the river one by one, so that they made a dam in the stormy water. Shantanu's heart went out to the child; and he hurried to protect him from danger.

At that moment Ganga, the Goddess, appeared and the child ran to her and stood by her. Shantanu recognized her at once. She smiled at him and held out the boy.

"This is your son, Shantanu," she said. "This is Devavrata and I have brought him back to you as I had said. Take him. Love him and look after him well, for he is born to be great."

She handed the boy over to Shantanu and then once again she disappeared. But this time Shantanu was not alone. His little son stood with him. Shantanu's heart overflowed with love for the child who stood beside him, looking up trustingly into his eyes.

"Come, my son," he said, "let us go back home," and he led the boy Devavrata to the royal palace.

This, people said, was the story of Devavrata's birth, and they were not surprised that Devavrata was so good and wise and handsome. for they knew him to be a heavenly being and the son of a Goddess.

Shantanu had grieved long years for the wife he had lost. But his heart rejoiced in his noble son. The boy grew up in the palace, and he was the light of his father's life, his pride and his joy. He was a grave, thoughtful lad who gave careful thought to every word that he spoke, and men knew they could trust him because he spoke only the truth. King Shantanu engaged many famous tutors to teach him and they found the boy eager for knowledge and quick to learn. In a short while he mastered all they had to teach, and yet he was never satisfied with his learning. He had an earnest mind that was always hungry for knowledge. As he grew up to be a tall and fine youth, he mastered every science and every skill and very early became learned in all the sacred writings. But he was a Kshatriya and a warrior above all, and it was as a warrior that Devavrata was best known; for there was none in the world who could send a surer arrow than he, and none so learned in the science of warfare. He was a true prince, and all his thoughts and all his actions were those worthy of a prince. He did nothing that was low or dishonest or cowardly; he was never mean and never jealous, and all men honoured him for his goodness and his noble heart. The fame of his courage spread far and wide, and there were many royal maidens who secretly prayed to have him as husband.

It was no wonder then that the people of

Hastinapura hailed Shantanu's choice with joy. They knew that the future of Hastinapura would be safe in the hands of one who was as noble and wise as Devavrata.

But one day, not long after Devavrata had been chosen heir-apparent, it happened that King Shantanu met a young and beautiful fisher girl, with whom he fell instantly in love and whom he wished to marry. When he sent messengers to her father, asking him for his daughter's hand in marriage, he found the shrewd old fisherman not at all easy to persuade. He received the King's offer coldly, without the enthusiasm Shantanu had expected him to show. It was all very well, the fisherman said, giving her to the king in marriage; but Shantanu was not young any more; he had not many years to live. What would happen to his daughter if Shantanu died and left her a widow? Who would care for her then? he wanted to know.

Back went the messengers to the royal palace and related everything to Shantanu. Shantanu decided to go himself and speak to the fisherman; he was quite infatuated with the fisher girl's beauty and wanted at all costs to marry her. But even though he was king, he fared no

14

better than his messengers had done. The fisherman had his own ideas about the matter. Shantanu's words fell on deaf ears, until at last the fisherman declared that he would allow the marriage only if Shantanu promised to make his daughter the principal Queen, and the son born to her his heirs. Having said this the fisherman refused to budge from his stand, though Shantanu tried to persuade him in many ways, promising him much money and many rewards. "The throne for my daughter and her descendants," said the old man stubbornly, "I cannot give her away for anything less."

Shantanu was very troubled. He had not expected this. How could he make the foolish promise the old man had asked for? How could he pass over Devavrata, who had been named heir-apparent and acclaimed by the people? Shantanu knew that there was not another in the world as good as Devavrata or as worthy to be king. So, greatly though Shantanu wanted to marry the fisher girl, Satyavati, he decided that he could not make the promise her father demanded. He left the fisherman and returned to the palace.

But he was sad. He could not forget her

beautiful face. Poor Shantanu grew thin and pale, pining for her. He began to neglect his kingly duties, and no longer took joy in the hunt. The palace minstrels and jesters could bring him no happiness. He became thin as a shadow.

Prince Devavrata watched his father anxiously. He loved him deeply and could not bear to see him suffer. He questioned the king's attendants and soon found out the reason for his father's unhappiness.

Then Devavrata went down to the riverside and sent for the fisherman. He spoke to him, begging from him the hand of Satyavati for his royal father. The fisherman spoke frankly: "When your father dies, Devavrata," he said, "Satyavati will not be queen. Your father is old and has not many years to live. What will become of Satyavati and her children after he dies? No, no, Devavrata; I cannot allow my daughter to be sacrificed in this manner. The king may have her only if he can promise me that he will make her his first queen and that her children and her children's children will inherit the throne. Only then will I consent to this marriage."

When Devavrata heard this, he exclaimed:

"But surely the king could easily have granted you this request!"

The fisherman's keen eyes searched the prince's. "How could the king promise this, O Devavrata?" he asked. "The throne is yours by right. How can the king give it away without your consent?" Then drawing closer to the youth, the fisherman whispered, his eyes shining with greed:

"But are *you* willing to agree to this, Devavrata? Are *you* willing to give up your throne for your father's happiness?"

Devavrata answered scornfully: "Do you think I lay store by such things as a throne? If it will make my father happy, O fisherman, I will gladly give it up." He held his head high, and his eyes were clear and did not flinch for an instant from the fisherman's gaze. The fisherman looked doubtful, and Devavrata swore to set his mind at rest: "O Fisherman," he said, holding up his right hand and speaking solemnly: "I, Prince Devavrata, give you my word of honour that Satyavati's children shall rule after Shantanu, and that I shall give up my claim to the royal throne." But the fisherman was not satisfied.

"Prince Devavrata," he said, "this is indeed

a great and noble thing you have done. But surely it is not enough. You are mortal, and one day you too will die. After you will come your sons and your sons' sons. Surely, Devavrata, they will not be bound by your word to me. Surely they will claim the throne which you have given up."

Devavrata looked at him calmly. Then he turned his eyes upon the blue waters of the river and stood lost in silent and deep thought. After a long while, he turned back to the fisherman and said, "O fisherman, I give you my word that I will never marry. Would this satisfy you?" His eyes were clear as he spoke, and his voice was steady. "With me shall my family end! And I shall have neither sons nor grandsons. You need have no fear."

In Devavrata's young face his eyes shone with a wonderful light. He stood in front of the fisherman, tall and straight and true, and made this great promise, giving up his own happiness. He would never know the joy of having a wife and family to love. All his life Devavrata would live alone. It was a great thing for a young man to promise for the sake of another. So great indeed was this promise, so great was this sacrifice which Devavrata had made,

that it is said that the heavens opened above
and the gods cried out "Bhishma!" and showered
flowers upon him. And ever after that Devavrata was known as Bhishma or "the one who
makes and keeps a great oath."

The fisherman was very pleased. He went
into his house and led out Satyavati, his daughter,
whom he handed over to the young prince.

Devavrata brought the fisher girl to Shantanu.
Then before the king and before the people of
the realm he repeated the solemn oath he had
taken upon the river bank—that he would
give up his claim to the throne and to the
kingdom and that he would never marry.
Thus he would remain childless throughout his
life. With him his family would end, and he
would have neither sons nor grandsons to
claim Shantanu's throne. Satyavati's descendants
would rule the kingdom of Bharata.

When he had repeated this great oath, his
father embraced him and loved him, and all
the world praised him. His father blessed him,
saying: "Live for ever, O noble prince. May you
live for ever. May you never know defeat, and
may you be so strong that death itself shall
not come to you, unless you wish it."

So it came about that Satyavati, the fisher

girl, was married to king Shantanu, and she bore him two sons Chitrangada and Vichitra-veerya. And after Shantanu they each in their turn came to the throne, and ruled the kingdom.

CHAPTER II

THE UNHAPPY PRINCESS

RUE to his word, Devavrata (or Bhishma as we shall now call him) renounced his claim to the throne of Hastinapura. He neither married nor had children. Instead, upon Shantanu's death, Bhishma placed the sons of Satyavati on the throne. Chitrangada, the elder son, did not rule long, for he met with an early death. When he died, his young brother Vichitraveerya succeeded him. Bhishma himself remained at the royal court, loyal and faithful to the king, his younger brother. He helped the young ruler to govern his kingdom, giving him wise advice. During this time there was peace in the land, for the fame of Bhishma's strength and skill in warfare had spread so wide and men so feared his might that the enemies of Hastinapura dared not attack it for fear of defeat.

One day there came news to the royal court of Hastinapura that the daughters of the ruler

of Kashi were to be given in marriage to who-
soever won them in battle. There was to be a
tournament in Kashi, in which all the royal
princes of the country could take part.

When Bhishma heard this, he decided to
go to Kashi and win the girls for his brother
Vichitraveerya, for they were famed for their
beauty. When he arrived there, he found
hundreds of princes had gathered already from
all parts of the land, for each prince had come
in the hope of winning glory for himself and
a beautiful princess for a bride.

They taunted Bhishma, for they thought he
had broken the vow he had made, and had
come to win a bride for himself. But Bhishma
said nothing. He took his seat among them and
when the signal was given, joined in the fierce
battle. And so skilled and excellent a warrior
was he that he overcame them all, one after
another, until there was no one left to challenge
him. Then, flushed with the pride of victory,
Bhishma came forward and lifting the three
beautiful princesses of Kashi into his chariot,
rode away with them towards Hastinapura.

He had not gone far when he was overtaken
by the young king Shalva who had come in
hot pursuit. He barred the way and challenged

Bhishma to battle, for he declared that Amba, the eldest of the three princesses, had been promised to him. Bhishma accepted the challenge, and a fierce fight took place in which once more Bhishma emerged victorious. Shalva drew back, his face dark with shame and anger. He entered his war-chariot and rode swiftly away, never once looking back, while Bhishma continued on his way to Hastinapura with the three beautiful trophies he had won.

Great were the rejoicings in Hastinapura over Bhishma's victories. Preparations were made for the marriage of Vichitraveerya to all the princesses. But there was one person who did not share in the happiness, and that was Amba: for Amba did not care for the weak and sickly Vichitraveerya, even though he was prince of Hastinapura. Her heart was set upon the young and handsome king Shalva. Ceaselessly she wept, and then at last she came before Bhishma and cried out to him in anger and sorrow:

"I cannot marry Vichitraveerya," she said, "for I do not love him. Shalva was chosen for my husband, and how can I marry another? You are famous for your righteousness, O Bhishma, and yet you keep a defenceless woman here against her will."

"What do you wish me to do, child?" Bhishma asked her gently, for he pitied her and wanted to help her. She answered without hesitation:

"Send me back to Shalva, for I was promised to him; that is the only thing to do, for it is right."

Bhishma realised the truth of her words and he sent her with attendants to Shalva's kingdom. But when they brought her before Shalva, he turned her away. For the sight of her brought to his mind his disgrace at the hands of Bhishma, and his heart grew bitter with anger.

"Why do you come here to me?" he asked her unkindly. "Do you feel no shame? Go back to him with whom you went!" And he told her he would never, never marry a girl who had been captured by a rival.

Amba stood dazed for a while. Then she turned away sorrowfully. Her heart wept at the shame that Shalva had brought upon her. With a heavy heart the poor girl returned to Hastinapura, with the attendants Bhishma had provided, and coming before him in tears she related her story to him.

"Shalva has turned me away," she wept. "What shall I do now?"

At the sight of the sorrowing girl Bhishma

felt guilty and troubled, for he knew that he was to blame for her unhappiness. He was anxious to do right by her, and help her out of her distress. So he brought her now before his young brother Vichitraveerya, who had married her two sisters, and advised him to take her for his wife. But Vichitraveerya refused, declaring scornfully that he did not want as a wife a girl who had given her heart to another.

Thus the proud Amba was refused a second time. Even Vichitraveerya, whom she despised, would not have her!

Amba turned to Bhishma. With tears in her eyes she now begged him to marry her.

"It is you who have brought this upon me," she cried. "You can make amends only by taking me as your wife."

Bhishma was deeply sorry for the poor, unhappy princess. But he was bound by his oath never to marry, and he could not break his word. Gently he explained this to the unhappy Amba.

"Go back to Shalva, child," he said. "Perhaps he could still be persuaded."

Amba had not much hope. Besides, how could she, a proud, royal princess, go back to someone who had already turned her away, and fall before him on her knees? But there was nothing else she could do. She swallowed her pride, and went to Shalva's country with a heavy heart.

Once more she came before Shalva and begged him to marry her. "I do not ask to be your chief wife. Let me be just one of your wives," she cried out to him. "Do not turn me away."

Shalva laughed scornfully.

"Never," he answered. "Never shall I marry a girl who was captured by another in battle and who has been the cause of my defeat and shame. Is one answer not good enough for you? Go back from where you have come!"

It seemed to Amba now that her cup of sorrow was full. The humiliation she had suffered on all sides made her heart bitter and angry. And she cursed her fate.

When she reached Hastinapura, she tried once more to persuade Bhishma to marry her.

But Bhishma shook his head and said:

"How can I break my word, O princess? How can I do a false thing?"

Amba covered her face with her hands and wept. Repulsed now on all sides, she began to brood upon her sorrow and loneliness. She was young and beautiful, a princess of royal blood;

yet her life had been blighted in the very bloom of her youth! Anger filled her heart against all the world, but especially against Bhishma, who, she felt, had brought all this shame and misery upon her.

Thoughts of revenge rose and swelled within her. It seemed to her that she would never find any peace until she had brought about Bhishma's death, and the thought began to haunt her like a fit of madness. Day by day she grew more desperate until she began to seek some way by which she could achieve her purpose.

She began to travel. She went from one kingdom to another, and begged the rulers to make war upon Bhishma. But they shook their heads and would have nothing to do with her, for they all feared Bhishma's strength. Trembling, they begged her to leave them. There was no one who would dare to face Bhishma in battle, and there was no one who would champion Amba's cause. With each failure the princess grew more bitter.

Her hatred for Bhishma was like a living thing inside her that was eating her heart away. It became the one important thing in her life. Nothing else seemed to matter. The world ceased to interest her. She took no joy in its beauty and in its goodness. Her eyes took on a wild crazed look.

"Revenge!" her heart cried out, "Revenge!"

One day she left the royal palace and retired into the forest. Since the world had failed her, she determined to seek the help of heaven. She spent many years in the forest living the hard life of a Sannyasini,[1] fasting and doing penance and torturing her body, until she who had been a young, laughter-loving princess became thin and old before her time. The joy of life went from her heart. Her face grew wrinkled and lined; her lovely soft eyes became harsh and her hands became coarse. Her long, glossy hair grew matted and brown with dust. But still this mattered little to her. For she lived only for revenge, praying for it day and night. For many years she lived on roots and fruits and berries. Then she ceased to eat even this, and began to live on water; as the years passed, she ceased to take even water, as she sat never moving, lost in her meditation.

So great was the power of her penance that

[1] Feminine of Sannyasi. A Sannyasi is an ascetic, a man who usually for religious reasons leads a life of severe self-discipline and hardships denying himself comforts and doing without material pleasures and enjoyment.

Nikhil Arun

Tripp Parent-Teacher
Conference Reminder

Date: Thursday, March 2nd

Time: 7:40-8:00

Teacher: Schmidt / Cutler

the day came at last when the Lord Shiva appeared before her and asked her what she desired.

"That Bhishma may be defeated and laid low," she cried out, "I wish that I may with my own hands bring about Bhishma's death for he has destroyed me!"

The Lord answered gently: "There is no one in the world, dear child, who can defeat Bhishma, for he is blessed by the Gods."

Then Amba cried out wildly: "Lord, is all my penance then in vain? Have I spent all these years for nothing then?"

Then Lord Shiva, who is also the great God of Destruction, gazed upon the unhappy woman with compassion in his eyes.

"Penance is never in vain, O Amba," he said. "And your desire shall be fulfilled. All men and everything that is born must die. That is the supreme law; and one day even Bhishma must die, for Bhishma is a mortal. But Bhishma is so good and so great and so pure that no ordinary death can touch him. Disease and old age will not hurt him; weapons will be of no avail against him. Only you can bring about Bhishma's death, O Amba, for you have spent all your life acquiring the strength for it by your penance and prayer.

Be at peace now, for the day will come when
you shall with your own hands bring about
Bhishma's death."

"How?" cried Amba impatiently, "Lord,
tell me how and when?" Then Shiva told her
that she would not do it in this life. Bhishma
was so pure and so powerful that for slaying
him she must take another birth. "You must
die first and be born again," said Shiva. "And
in your next life you shall be born as the daughter
of King Drupada of Panchala and be the cause
of Bhishma's death."

"In my next life," she echoed. "Lord, how
can I wait so long? And then how would I
know that these things will truly come to pass?"

The Lord smiled gravely to see her impatience.
"See," he said, removing from around his
throat the string of *rudraksha* beads and putting
them around her neck. "These beads shall be
your sign." And he left her.

Amba's withered heart stirred and rejoiced.
She got up and leaving the forest, she made her
way to Kampilya, Drupada's capital city and
to his royal palace. Here on the gatepost she
hung the beads that were around her neck,
and then she made her way into the palace
past the astonished guards who gazed terror-
30

stricken at her gaunt, ochre-clad figure. Into
the sacrificial hall she came where Drupada
was performing a sacrifice. He hoped by his
sacrifice to please the gods so that they would
bless him with children. The orange flames of
the sacrificial fire crackled and leaped up to
the rafters. The priests chanted as they fed it.
Amba stood there and stared. As she did so a
strange look came into her eyes. The assembled
people heard a cry escape her. Then as they
looked on amazed, they saw the figure in orange
dart across the room and leap into the flames.
In a second they had consumed Amba and
there was nothing left of her but ash. So Amba
died. But it was only her mortal body that died.
Her desire did not die. It lived on strong as
ever, and because of it Amba took birth again.
And as Shiva had promised, she was born as
the daughter of Drupada, King of Panchala.

The princess grew up in her father's royal
palace. They named her Shikhandini. She was
a strange silent child, dark and secretive. Often
she wandered alone, deep in her melancholy
thoughts which she shared with no one. One
day as she went out past the palace gates,
Shikhandini found on the door-post the necklace
of beads that Amba had left there. The child

31

streched out her hand and reached for it. She
put it around her neck and as soon as she had
done so she remembered the past,—all Amba's
sorrows and her all-consuming desire for revenge. Her former life returned to her, and she
began to remember the purpose of the birth
she had now taken. And now she was seized
with a quiet determination. Once again she who
had been Amba began to pray and to meditate.
Strange was Shikhandini's prayer, for this time
she prayed that she might be changed into a man.

Her prayer was granted to her. For in the
forest the princess Shikhandini found a Yaksha[1]
who agreed to exchange his manhood for her
womanhood. Thus Shikhandini returned to
Drupada's palace changed into a man.

And now her restless heart was at peace at
last; for, after many years, she knew in a strange
way that the wrongs Amba had suffered would
be avenged and that Bhishma would meet his
end at last.

Many years were to pass before this would
happen, and for the present we must leave
this child of fate, and turn to the household
of yet another princess of the time, and the
happenings around her.

[1] A semi-divine spirit, servant of the gods.

CHAPTER III

THE COMING OF KARNA

NE golden morning a young princess sat at her window gazing at the eastern sky. The sun was rising, and the earth was stirring to life at his magic touch. The sky was all crimson and gold; the dewdrops hung glinting like diamonds from the leaves, and all the birds were singing. It seemed to the young girl that she had never seen anything more beautiful in her life than the Sun God, who rode across the sky in his golden chariot. As she thought this, she remembered a prayer charm that a sage had once given her. By the power of this charm, the sage had said, she could call the very gods in the heavens to her side, and they would come at her bidding, and she would be the mother of their sons. The princess whose name was Kunti wondered what would happen if she uttered the charm now. Would the Sun God really come? She had never used the charm before, for she was still very young.

Her heart beat fast at the thought of seeing the Sun God, and she trembled. Then timidly, not quite believing she whispered the magic words. She held her breath, scared by what she had done, for she knew it had not been right for her to utter the charm before she was quite grown up. She did not want any sons, at least not yet. She knew she was too young.

But even as she was thinking these things she saw the shining God of the Sun descending in a great blaze of gold. The next minute he was beside her and his eyes looked upon her with love.

Kunti trembled with fear. She covered her face with her hands and begged him to go back to the Heavens, from where he had come. But this the Sun God could not do, for he was held by the power of the magic charm she had uttered. The Sun God loved Kunti greatly, and when he returned to his kingdom in the sky, she became the mother of his little son upon the earth—a beautiful, shining child, bright like the Sun God himself. And because he was the Sun God's baby, he was not like other babies: even at birth he wore armour which *shone like gold, and strange ear-rings in his* ears which glowed with a redddish light.

But Kunti was not happy. She knew that Kuntibhoja, her father and the people around her would be angry with her, and she wished she had never met the Sun God nor borne the child. She would have liked to hide the baby away, but that was not possible. Full of fear, she thought at last of a plan by which she could get rid of it. One night she placed the child in a wooden box and hurried out of the palace gates with it. She came to a river, and there she set the box afloat upon the water. Then she hurried back to the palace. But her heart was heavy at the thought of what she had done. She knew that as long as she lived, she would never have any peace or happiness, for the memory of the innocent little baby which she had set afloat upon the river would be with her always.

Days passed and Kunti grew into a beautiful young woman, but her eyes remained sad and she rarely smiled. Gone was her laughter, gone were her gay, girlish ways. Often she wept to herself at night thinking about the wooden box upon the river. But she told no one, and the secret lay locked up in her sad heart.

When the time came for it, she was given in marriage to Pandu, the second son of Vichitra-

One night she placed the child in a wooden box...

veerya of Hastinapura, and Ambika. Vichitraveerya was dead, and his eldest son, Dhritarashtra was blind. The elder statesmen of the
kingdom, among whom was Bhishma, had
therefore placed Pandu upon the throne of
Hastinapura to rule in Dhritarashtra's place.
Kunti lived in the royal palace. She served
her elders dutifully and won the love of all
around her. But no one knew the sad, dark
secret that lay heavy like lead upon her heart,
and all her life she lived under its grim and
terrible shadow.

But Kunti's baby son, who had so cruelly
been abandoned, was not fated to die. The
wooden chest that carried him floated down the
river with the current, and after a while came
near to Hastinapura. As it drifted, it was seen
and hauled ashore by a man who had happened
at that moment to be upon the bank. This man
was Adiratha, a humble charioteer of Hastinapura. He was greatly surprised to see the baby
inside the chest, but when he lifted it up and
saw its shining beauty he was filled with a great
joy.

Adiratha took the little baby home to his
wife, Radha. She heard the story he had to
tell, and her eyes filled with grateful happy

tears, for Radha had no children of her own, and had always longed for them. Now it seemed that Heaven had answered her prayer in a strange manner.

Radha and Adiratha decided to adopt the little foundling. They named him Karna, because of the wonderful rings in his ears. They knew in their simple hearts that he could not have been an ordinary child, for no ordinary child had ear-rings such as this one wore. No ordinary child was encased, as this one was, in armour—a coat of mail that shone like gold.

Under their loving care, Karna grew up to be a handsome, tall youth. His eyes were full of a glowing light and his mouth was proud. He was quick and clever in his ways, and early in life he learned to draw the bow and wield the sword; and so skilful was he in the use of weapons that the good, simple charioteer and his wife and all who saw him were filled with wonder. There was no other boy around like him.

He spoke little and kept his deep, melancholy thoughts to himself. And yet he was always upright in his dealings, faithful, generous and bold. He scorned anything that was low or mean or deceitful. They found him quick-tempered, and when he was roused to anger his dark eyes flashed and his face flushed, and his hand trembled upon the hilt of his sword. But he was as quick to forgive and forget, and he would never betray a friend, nor break a promise nor forget a kindness done to him.

And so, though men feared him, and though many secretly hated him for his quick anger, there were others who admired him in their hearts and loved him for his generous nature.

But no one, not even his foster parents, knew the story of his birth, nor of his immortal father, the Sun God, nor of his mother, the beautiful Kunti, queen of Hastinapura.

CHAPTER IV

THE PANDAVA PRINCES

ING Pandu of Hastinapura ruled the State wisely and well. Around him were many experienced and able counsellors. Of them all, the two ablest were Bhishma, his uncle and Vidura his half-brother. Vidura was born of a humble slave girl but he had grown to be wise and rich in understanding. Pandu took their advice on all matters, and Hastinapura during Pandu's reign was like a strong sailing-ship which was guided by a trusty captain and manned by faithful sailors. King Pandu had married Kunti and Madri, and the two wives loved each other dearly. All went well and the days passed peacefully, until a sickness attacked King Pandu. Because of this he retired to the forest with his wives. For many years they lived there, while the blind Dhritarashtra returned as regent to his place on the throne. The Pandava princes were born while Pandu and Kunti lived in the forest.

The Pandava Princes

The five Pandavas were not ordinary children. They were the gifts of the gods and when they were born they shone with a heavenly light. Yudhishthira the eldest, was given by Dharma the Lord of Justice, who is also the God of Death; and Indra who was the king of the gods gave to Kunti the brave and noble Arjuna; the valiant Bhima was the gift of the Wind God, Vayu, while Nakula and Sahadeva came to Madri from the Ashwini twins. They grew up in their forest home; and Pandu, who with each passing day grew weaker and paler because of his illness, was full of joy to see them before him.

But Pandu did not live long, and his sons were still children when one day he died suddenly. The two queens were grief-stricken. They gathered their fatherless boys around them and mourned for their husband.

The Rishis who lived in the forest hurried to their side to comfort them. They went to Hastinapura with the sad news. Madri's sorrow was so great that when they lighted the funeral pyre of Pandu, she entered the flames and ended her life. Her two little sons she entrusted to Kunti.

Kunti gathered the children to her. She was

dressed now in the white garments of a widow. Her beautiful face was lined with sorrow, her eyes ringed with dark lines. Fear was in her heart as she looked upon the five orphans; the days ahead would not be easy any more. The Rishis advised her to take her sons and go back to the ancestral home in Hastinapura where it was right and natural for them to be.

Bhishma, Vidura and the other elders of the realm who had hurried to the forest on hearing the news of the king's death, also begged Kunti to go back with them to Hastinapura. And so with her sons the widowed queen followed the elders to the capital city.

As they approached it, they could see its golden roof-tops gleaming in the sun. Great crowds of people had gathered to receive them and welcome them. And though there was grief in their faces for the beloved king who was dead, there was pride and joy too in their eyes as they looked at the five noble princes. The people whispered to one another: "God bless the sons of Pandu; they are good and noble. They are handsome as the very gods in the Heavens."

Now when these words reached the sons of Dhritarashtra, they were not pleased at all.

The Pandava Princes

There were a hundred of them, and they were
called the Kauravas. Duryodhana was the eldest.
He was a proud and haughty boy, and he was
not entirely happy about his cousins. When
Duryodhana heard what the people of Hastinapura said about them he frowned darkly. His
eyes clouded over, and the canker of jealousy
began to stir in his heart. He knew he was
expected to receive his cousins and welcome
them. It was a bitter thought, and he ground
his teeth as he went down the palace steps towards them. He hated them, and it angered
him to see the love the people showed them; it
tortured him to see the joy and pride on the
faces of Bhishma and Vidura. Everybody praised
them! Oh, it was a bitter day for Duryodhana,—
this day of the Pandavas' return to Hastinapura.
But he swallowed his anger and held out his
hand. He smiled and called them his brothers;
he embraced them and led them up the palace
steps, hating them secretly all the while. The
blind king Dhritarashtra tottered up to them
and when they bent down and touched his
feet, the old man raised them to him and embraced them. Then Gandhari held out her
arms to them. Gandhari was Dhritarashtra's
wife and the mother of Kauravas. So great was

her love and devotion to her blind husband that from the day that she had married him, Gandhari had bound up her own eyes with a cloth and refused to see the loveliness of the world because she could not share it with him. Gandhari embraced the sobbing Kunti and spoke to her many words of comfort. She gathered the Pandava princes to her with love and kindness. And all the time Duryodhana watched, a smile upon his lips, but within his heart the beginnings of new jealousies and hatreds, the beginnings of restless ambition and envy, that were, with the passing days, to spread and swell until they consumed him, and brought him to his ruin.

CHAPTER V

DRONA

KUNTI and her sons lived in the royal palace at Hastinapura, and the Pandava and Kaurava princes grew up together. The head of the household was their great uncle Bhishma and his word was law. He loved the boys as if they were his own sons; so did Vidura, Dhritarashtra's half brother. Kunti watched anxiously as her sons grew. Vague fears for their safety haunted her, for she knew that the Kauravas had no love for them. She did not trust the Kauravas. And yet she knew that while Bhishma was there she had nothing to fear, for Bhishma was wise and just in all his dealings.

The princes ran about the palace and played together; they sported in the palace gardens. They played with their ball and flew kites. They had marbles and catapults and slings, and, like the Kshatriyas they were, they had their little bows and arrows and swords.

One day while the princes of Hastinapura were playing together as usual, their ball, thrown far and fast by one of them, fell into an old well in a corner of the compound. The boys gathered round the well and peered into it. They could see the ball, but had no idea how to get it out.

As they stood there trying to decide what to do, they saw walking towards them a little dark-skinned man, a stranger whom they had never seen before. He had keen sharp eyes like needle points, which seemed to pierce them through and through. They knew him to be a Brahmin because of the sacred thread around his body.

The stranger came up to them and asked them what the matter was, and the boys were glad to tell him of their trouble.

"We have lost our ball," they chorused together, "It fell into the well while we were playing and now we cannot get it out!" The dark stranger smiled.

"Surely that is not a difficult task for boys so well trained in archery as you are," he remarked, and his eyes seemed to mock them. They looked at him surprised, and not a little amused.

"Archery?" they asked laughing. "What has

Surely that is not a difficult task for boys so well
trained in archery as you!

archery got to do with getting a ball out of a well, Brahmin?"

"Everything," the stranger answered, smiling mysteriously. "Everything as you will see now. Get me an arrow!" But the princes had no arrows ready that day. "No matter," said the stranger. "Go, get me from the field beyond, a few good strong stems of Khusha grass growing there, and I will show you such a sight as you have never seen before."

His voice seemed to command them, and they sped off quickly in the direction in which he pointed and did as they were told. Then they came running back and stood breathlessly around him watching him carefully. He chose the longest and strongest of the grass stems. Then uttering his prayer charm he shot it. The grass stem went whizzing into the well with the speed of lightning. It went in such a manner that it struck the ball and caused it to bound out of the water and strike the wall of the well, then bounce back off the side, up in the air. The Brahmin caught it neatly and deftly, and handed it back to the astonished boys. It was a remarkable feat and they stared at him in wonder. Then Yudhishthira, still dazed with his astonishment, said: "O Brahmin, there is

a ring too, in the well—one that I lost some
days ago. When the waters settle you will be
able to see it at the bottom. Can you get it out
for me as you did the ball?"

"Nothing easier!" laughed the stranger. He
picked up the bow and chose another stem.
This time he cut a deep notch into it. That
done, he drew his bow and shot the grass stem
down into the well. Once more the boys saw
it speeding down. They saw it strike the earth
through the ring so that it was caught in the
notch. The stem stuck in the mud and stood
upright. Then the man sent the other grass
stems one after another, carefully cutting
notches into each. So well were the grasses
aimed and with such precision and power, that
each grass struck the notch of the one sent
before it and stuck fast in it. Thus, he sent his
grasses one by one into the well, and they made
a long line of arrows and he was able to reach
for the ring, and get it out.

"Bravo!" cried the delighted princes, and
they stared at him in admiration. "You are
truly a great archer. What is your name,
stranger?" But the stranger only shook his
head and smiled to see their wonder.

"Go!" he commanded them. "Go and tell

the grand sire what you have seen today." The princes needed no second bidding. They ran off and breathlessly reported to Bhishma all that had happened. When Bhishma heard their story he knew at once that this man who had come to their palace was no ordinary archer. He had heard of Dronacharya, the son of Bharadwaja, who, it was said, had learnt his archery from the gods in the heavens. Bhishma was sure that the stranger in the garden was no other than this same Drona. He hurried down to the garden with the boys and met the mysterious archer. He found that his guess had been correct and he was full of joy. For Bhishma knew that there was no one in the land of Bharata who could equal Drona as an archer.

He forthwith engaged him to teach the royal princes. From then on Drona lived at the royal palace at Hastinapura and taught the princes the arts of warfare.

Drona proved an excellent teacher. It is said that one day he called his pupils to him to test their powers of concentration. He gathered them around him and pointed out a target. It was a bird on the branch of a tree. "Bring down the head of the bird for me!" commanded Drona, and he told Yudhishthira to come for-

Drona

ward alone because he was the eldest. Yudhishthira drew his bow. But at that moment Drona
held up his hand: "Wait!" he said, "Tell me
first, what do you see?" "I see the bird," answered
Yudhishthira, "and the branch on which it
sits and the leaves of the tree."

"Go on," Drona commanded. "Is there anything else? Tell me." Yudhishthira answered,
"I see the tree and sky and you, my teacher,
and I see my brothers."

Then Drona said to him: "Stand aside. You
have still much to learn."

After Yudhishthira came Duryodhana. He
answered Drona's question just as Yudhishthira
had done, saying that he saw the bird and the
branch, the leaves and the tree, the sky and
before him, his teacher and beyond, his brothers.
Then Drona set him aside also, and asked for
Bhima. Bhima did no better. At that Drona
was full of sorrow that his pupils had not been
as good as he wished. At last he called Arjuna
to him, and repeated his questions.

"Do you see the bird?"

"I do," Arjuna answered.

"And what else besides?"

"I see only the bird," Arjuna answered.
"Nothing else."

51

"Do you not see the tree and the sky and the earth, myself, your teacher, and beyond, do you not see your brothers?"

"I see only the bird," Arjuna repeated.

Arjuna's answer pleased Drona, for this was what he was hoping to hear from his students. He then asked again, "What part of the bird do you see, Arjuna?"

Arjuna answered: "Only the head!" Drona walked up to Arjuna and patted him on his back. "Lower your bow, O Arjuna," he exclaimed. "You have proved yourself the true archer. For, above everything an archer must be undivided in his attention; when the true archer concentrates, his eyes see nothing but his target, and his arrow will reach it unerringly."

Ever afterwards Drona loved Arjuna as his star pupil. After a few months of training, Drona wished to test his pupils again. At the same time he longed to punish Drupada, King of Panchala, for a wrong done to him many years before. Many years back, Drupada, prince of Panchala, and Drona had studied under Drona's father, Bharadwaja, in the latter's hermitage. Those had been the happy, carefree days of their youth, and during that time the prince

Drona

of Panchala and the poor Brahmin boy had
sworn eternal friendship. At the end of his
course of studies Drupada prepared to return
to Panchala. The royal chariot awaited him
and servants and attendants bent low before
him. As Drupada walked up to the chariot he
could not help feeling that he was above everybody there in rank and status. Nevertheless he
embraced his friend Drona warmly and invited
him to come to Panchala. Drona had promised
to go. Drupada returned to Panchala, and
inheriting its throne, was crowned its king.

For many years, however, Drona was not
able to keep his promise to visit his friend. He
was continuing his studies, gaining mastery
over all the sciences and arts of the time. He
was an earnest young man, and he proved to
be an apt pupil: it was said that the gods had
blessed him with the knowledge of divine
weapons and with the secrets of using them.
In course of time this earnest and serious young
scholar married the sister of Kripacharya, the
instructor to the Pandava and Kaurava princes
at Hastinapura, and his wife bore him a little
son.

And now a new phase began in Drona's life.
Until then Drona had not cared for material

comfort or for wealth, and had been content to
live a stern, harsh life in his forest hermitage.
But the birth of his son changed all this. The
boy became the centre of his life. Drona longed
to give his son all the material comforts he had
never wanted for himself. So he determined to
find work for himself at one of the royal courts,
so that for the sake of his son he might earn
his living and improve his condition. Then he
remembered his boyhood friend, Drupada, who
was now king of the Panchala kingdom, and he
made up his mind to go to Drupada's court
and seek his help. As an old friend, Drupada
would surely come to his aid.

But when Drona, barefooted and dressed
only in his loin cloth, came before Drupada on
his throne, he found the king very different
from the boyhood friend he had known. For
wealth and power had gone to Drupada's head
and he had grown proud and haughty. He
looked at the poor Brahmin before him, and
was ashamed to own that once they had been
friends. In that great royal court, in the presence
of all assembled there, Drupada insulted Drona.
His lip curled with scorn: "Friends!" he exclaimed, "I do not remember ever having
known you. Get you gone, Brahmin, and if it

is alms you want, go to the alms house, where rice is given to beggars."

Drona looked up in surprise and grief. "I have not come for alms, Drupada," he said, and he reminded Drupada of the happy days of their youth. But the haughty king refused to acknowledge that they had once been friends. "You are no better than a common beggar!" he said. "Friendship is possible only between equals. How can a beggar claim a king's friendship? Please leave the royal court at once. We have seen thousands of your kind begging for scraps from rich men's tables, and we have no time for people like you." The servants laid rough hands on him and Drona was turned out of the court.

Drona felt utterly humiliated. Anger filled his heart. He went to live in the house of his brother-in-law, Kripacharya in Hastinapura. There he brooded upon the wrongs he had suffered. It was while he was there that he attracted the notice of Bhishma and was engaged by him to be tutor to the royal princes.

Drona never forgot Drupada's insulting behaviour. He never forgave him and he longed for revenge.

When he felt that the Hastinapura princes

had been trained enough, he called Duryodhana to him and commanded him to make war on the Panchala king and to capture him. Duryodhana obeyed. But Drupada defeated him and Duryodhana came back in disgrace. Then Drona named Arjuna for the task and sent him to Panchala.

Arjuna went and defeated the Panchalas and captured their king. At Arjuna's command Drupada was brought before Drona; his pride was brought to the dust, and Drona's desire for revenge was satisfied. Drona reminded the royal captive of the time when he had said to him that friendship was possible only between equals. "You can have half the kingdom back, Drupada," said Drona, smiling contemptuously. "The other half I shall keep for myself. So shall I be king and your equal; so may I claim your friendship." Drupada winced at the mocking voice in which these words were said. His desire for revenge fulfilled, Drona ordered Drupada to be set free and allowed him to return to his own country. The proud king bowed before Drona. But in his heart he began now to hate him.

Humbled and smarting under the disgrace of his defeat, it was now Drupada's turn to plan revenge. He hated to think that he owed his throne to Drona's generosity. With his heart burning inside him, he began to pray.

He prayed that he might have a son who would one day bring about Drona's death, and a daughter who would one day be Arjuna's wife. For during the journey to Hastinapura, Drupada had been struck by Arjuna's noble bearing, by his wisdom and goodness. Drupada's prayers were answered, and there were born to him the dark twins, Dhrishtadyumna and Krishna. Many years later, the princess Krishna who is known as Draupadi, the daughter of Drupada, was to win the hand of the Pandava princes in marriage. And many years later still Dhrishtadyumna, on the field of battle, was to bring about Drona's death. But these events were all hidden in the future. Just now everything seemed peaceful in the land of Bharata. The angers smouldering inside the hearts of men lay hidden like venomous snakes beneath the ground.

CHAPTER VI

A WICKED PLOT

UNTI'S fears were not without ground. The Pandavas and the Kauravas grew up together and shared all things equally. But there was no love lost between them. Duryodhana and his brothers hated the five Pandavas. They looked upon them as rivals and intruders, and wished that they had never come to live in Hastinapura at the royal palace. They were jealous of the Pandavas and the love that the people bore them. They envied their good looks and noble bearing. They noticed that by their charm and good manners and their friendliness, the Pandavas made themselves popular among all, and they feared that the people of Hastinapura would, upon Dhritarashtra's death, choose Yudhishthira, the eldest of them all, to be king and pass Duryodhana by. Duryodhana nursed hatred in his heart, but outwardly he pretended a love and friendship for his cousins which he was far from feeling.

Whenever he got a chance, he tried to harm them, and once he even tried to kill Bhima.

Bhima was Duryodhana's special enemy. Bhima was a big, strong, simple-hearted boy with a curious sense of humour. He had a turn for practical jokes and he played them upon the Kauravas to their great annoyance. The Kauravas were vain, pompous youths, and Bhima for his part disliked them as heartily as they disliked him. He took it upon himself to bring down their pride. He was something of a bully too, and secretly Duryodhana feared his great strength. It happened that once Bhima, seeing Duryodhana upon a tree stealing fruit, went up to the tree and shook it violently, threatening to uproot it, till Duryodhana, white-faced and trembling, clung to the branches and begged him to stop. Bhima seemed to think this extremely funny!

Another time he ducked the Kaurava brothers one by one into the icy waters of a river, holding them by the scruff of their necks till each one spluttered and shivered and cried out for mercy.

Often he would engage in wrestling bouts with his cousins, who were like toys in hands. He would throw them down with ease, one after the other, and would walk away roaring with laughter.

This, of course, did not make Bhima popular with his cousins. Duryodhana's hatred for him increased each day. Deep in his heart, Duryodhana nursed a desire to kill Bhima; but Bhima was too strong for him, and Duryodhana knew he had no chance against his cousin in an open fight. So day and night Duryodhana plotted against the unsuspecting Bhima.

Then at last one day, when his plans were ripe, he approached the Pandavas, suggesting that they should all go out and camp for a few days on the near-by river bank. The unsuspecting Pandavas readily agreed, and the party set out in high spirits for the royal summer house on the river bank. Here they spent several happy days, swimming, boating, riding and hunting. On the last night of their stay Duryodhana arranged a feast, at which all the choicest dishes that the Pandava brothers loved were set before them. It was a royal feast and Bhima, who loved good food, fell to it with a royal appetite. For him Duryodhana had had special food cooked and Bhima ate vast quantities of it. Duryodhana watched him closely and was very pleased. *For the special food was poisoned.* Duryodhana had had Bhima's food poisoned!

That night, while the Pandava princes slept, Duryodhana and his brothers came to Bhima where he lay in a deep, death-like slumber, the effect of the poisoned food. Quickly and silently they bound him with ropes and carried him out; they flung him into the river, and returned to the palace as if nothing had happened.

The next morning there was a search for Bhima; but when he was nowhere to be found, the Pandavas, thinking he had gone off somewhere by himself, and believing that he would return, went back to Hastinapura with their cousins. Only Duryodhana and his close friends knew, and they rubbed their hands with glee and secretly rejoiced, believing that at last Bhima was dead. But Bhima was not dead. He was too strong for any poison to kill him. It had only made him unconscious. He fell into a deep whirlpool in the water and was sucked into it. Deeper and deeper he went until he reached the kingdom of the snakes that was under the river. Now the snake-people are wise, gentle creatures with a vast knowledge of poisons and medicines. They gathered around him as he lay still and unconscious; and when they saw his handsome, noble form they took pity on him and with their double tongues they sucked out the poison from his body until he revived and sat up, dazed and bewildered. Then the snakes spoke to him and questioned him and when they heard his story they nodded gravely:

"This is Duryodhana's doing," they said. "Duryodhana and his brothers hate you. They will try every means to kill you."

Bhima stayed with the snake-people for a while until he had recovered his strength. They would have liked him to stay with them for ever, and begged him to do so. But to this Bhima would not agree, for he loved his mother and brothers too much to allow himself to go from them.

So he thanked the kindly creatures for their goodness and help; and after he had grown strong and healthy on the nourishing foods they gave him, he wished them good-bye, and returned to Hastinapura.

Duryodhana and his brothers were amazed to see Bhima back looking well and happy. They had never doubted that their evil plan had succeeded. Kunti too and her other sons had waited anxiously for him and then sorrowfully had given him up for dead and ceased to hope

for his coming. When Bhima returned, therefore, their joy was unbounded. The Kauravas
came and greeted him too, with smiles upon
their faces. But in their hearts they were worried
because their plot had failed. Bhima, however,
gave no sign that he knew of the plot to murder
him. Duryodhana smiled unsteadily, wondering
secretly how much Bhima might have found out.
But he too gave no sign of what went on in his
mind.

That night Bhima told his brothers and his
mother the story. They spoke in whispers
because now they knew what danger they were
in. They agreed that they must be very careful.
Whatever they did, Duryodhana and his brothers
hated them and would stop at nothing to harm
them. They knew that they had powerful
enemies in that beautiful palace and things
were never what they appeared to be. A smile
might mean that a plot was hatching. Soft words
might be like double-edged swords. A goblet of
sparkling wine might contain death, and behind
the sculptured pillars of the palace murder might
be lurking. They could not be too careful.

So the days passed, filled with suspicion and
fear, and in the palace, the children of Pandu and
the children of Dhritarashtra grew to manhood.

CHAPTER VII

EKALAVYA

KALAVYA was the son of the chief of a tribe called the Nishadas who lived in the forests and made their living by hunting and fishing. Ekalavya had grown up in his forest home and had become a brave, strong and worthy youth. As he grew up he longed to learn the skills of Kshatriya warfare, but there was no one to teach him. He had heard about the great Drona who lived in Hastinapura and whom none could equal as a teacher. Ekalavya determined to be Drona's pupil and learn from him. So he left his forest home and journeyed to the distant Hastinapura.

It was a long and difficult journey, but it did not daunt Ekalavya. After many days of walking he reached the great city at last and the gates of the royal palace. In the gardens a little dark man was instructing his pupils. Ekalavya saw how they listened to him with awe and respect. He noticed how clear his

instructions were and how he commanded their
attention by his authority. And he knew that
this man could be no other than the great
teacher, Drona. Then the youth advanced and
coming before the teacher where he was teaching
his pupils, knelt before him and saluted him.
Drona returned the greetings, wondering who
the lad was. He saw with pleasure how tall
and straight-limbed the kneeling youth was,
and how clear his eyes, shining as they did with
the light of intelligence. Drona asked him who
he was and what he wanted, and when he
heard how the boy had come asking to be his
pupil, the teacher smiled as he felt flattered, and
said:

"What is your caste, child? What is your
family? Where were you brought up?"

"We are Nishadas, Sir," Ekalavya answered.
"My father is chief of the Nishadas tribe, and
we live in the forests. I belong therefore to no
caste, for our people do not belong to the Aryan
race. I long to learn the martial arts and to be
a soldier in the service of my country."

"A forest tribesman!" At these words Drona
drew himself up haughtily exclaiming, "Do you
not know, boy, that I am a teacher of Kshatriya
princes? I do not teach tribesmen; I take only

Kshatriyas for my pupils. Please go away, young man, for I cannot teach you."

Ekalavya walked out of the garden and stood gazing at Drona's royal pupils for a while. It was a bitter disappointment to him. He had come to Hastinapura with only one purpose— to become a pupil of the renowned teacher, and he had been rebuffed. He walked away deep in thought and sad at heart. He did not feel any anger at Drona's refusal. Indeed, his desire to learn was so great that he had no time at all to waste on anger. The more he thought about it the stronger became Ekalavya's desire to be Drona's pupil and learn from him. But of course Drona would not change his mind.

Ekalavya returned to the forest from where he had come. When he arrived there he continued to think, until at last he found a solution to his problem. He set to work with clay, and made himself an image in the likeness of Drona. He set up this clay image and meditated deeply before it. In his heart he looked upon this image as Drona himself the teacher. And after he had meditated for a long time, he got up and began to practise the art of the soldier, shooting his arrows at targets that he set up for himself. Every day he did this alone in the forest, pray-

ing before the clay image and studying and
practising before it with such concentration and
deep intent, that it was not long before he
mastered in the lonely forest, the skills that Drona
taught the princes in the royal palace in Hastinapura. And far from feeling anger at the insult_
he had suffered at Drona's hands, he felt for
Drona a deep love and reverence, for he looked
upon him as a teacher in spite of the latter's
contemptuous attitude.

One day Drona, in order to teach his royal
pupils hunting, brought them into a forest. It
happened to be the same one where Ekalavya
lived, but Drona did not know this.

As the royal party made their way into the
forest, Drona noticed signs that made him feel
that they were not alone here. There were arrows
stuck fast in the tree trunks as if someone had
been practising archery. There were tracks and
footmarks. He was still wondering about the
discovery when one of his dogs began to bark.
At that moment, there came swiftly through
the air, one after another, seven shining arrows
with the speed of lightning and struck the dog's
opened mouth. Drona could see that they had
been shot from a great distance, and whoever
had shot them, had taken aim with nothing to

guide him except the sound of the dog's barking. They were the arrows of a true warrior.

The sight surprised Drona very much, for he had always believed that there was no one who could equal the students he had trained. Now he was not so sure. He wondered who the unknown warrior could be, and spurred on by his curiosity he made his way into the forest, bidding his pupils to follow him.

And when they had gone some way into the forest they came upon Ekalavya in a small clearing, standing with his bow drawn and his arrow ready to fly. The youth looked up and saw them. Instantly he put his bow to one side, and folding his hands together, went down on his knees. Drona wondered greatly at his noble bearing and conduct. "Here," he thought, "is a true Kshatriya, one who would make the world proud that he had been born!"

"Who are you, young man?" Drona asked. "And who is your teacher? Surely your teacher must be a great Guru to have trained such a mighty warrior as you!"

"I am Ekalavya, Sir," the youth answered. "My family belongs to the Nishadas tribe and we live in the forests. My teacher is the great and incomparable Drona."

Drona started.

"Drona?" he repeated, looking upon the kneeling boy, bewildered. "But Drona lives in Hastinapura. He knows no Ekalavya!" Drona had forgotton the incident that had taken place in the palace garden. Then Ekalavya told how he had made the clay image of the Teacher and, looking upon it as the living Drona, had sat before it in prayer and practised the martial arts in its living presence. "Though he does not know it, Drona is in truth my Guru!" he concluded.

"A clay image?" Drona whispered and suddenly he remembered the youth he had turned away. He was filled with wonder and astonishment and a deep pleasure in spite of himself. But as he stood there with the kneeling boy before him, troubled feelings of envy and fear began to arise in Drona's heart, though he allowed no sign of them to show upon his face. He spoke with a smile. "I have come before you in person, O Ekalavya. I am your teacher, Drona, and I wish to test your skill. Let there be a contest here and now, so that your skill can be matched with that of the Kshatriya princes of Hastinapura who are also my pupils." Nothing could have made Ekalavya happier. Joyfully he agreed to Drona's suggestion. The contest started. There in the forest glade the pupils of Drona displayed their skill one by one before the master. Yudhishthira, Duryodhana and Bhima, Arjuna and Dushasana, and all those who had learnt from Drona, came forward to wrestle and fence and shoot their arrows at targets that he named. But of them all Ekalavya was easily the best, and there was no one, not even Arjuna who could excel the forest tribesman. One by one, they retired, defeated by him, filled with shame and jealousy. He alone remained fresh and smiling and clear-eyed, eager and ready for more.

Drona looked round at the royal pupils whom he had trained with such care; he could not bear to think that this forest tribesman whom he had turned away and refused to teach, had proved their superior. Not one of them could match him. Drona felt bitterly disappointed. But he swallowed his feelings and smiled at the boy. He called him to his side.

"Since I am your teacher and have taught you all you know, I must have my fees. A teacher must be paid."

"That he must!" agreed Ekalavya, "Whatever my teacher asks I shall give to him."

Drona looked at him keenly, while Ekalavya continued, "My teacher has only to command me, and all I have is his."

"Then listen, Ekalavya," said Drona, and he did not for a moment take his eyes from that eager, young face, "In return for my teaching I will take from you your right thumb."

The boy started slightly. Drona wished to maim him, so that he could never draw his bow again as well as he did. With Ekalavya maimed, Drona's Kshatriya pupils would have no rival, and Arjuna would have no match. Ekalavya understood this, but he smiled gently.

"What my teacher asks I will gladly give," he said. He drew his sword and with one stroke he cut off his right thumb. The bleeding offering he made to Drona his teacher with a smiling face and an ungrudging heart.

Ekalavya's story is a sad one. It is the story of a great wrong and injustice done to one who was noble and brave and true. But the Mahabharata tells of men who lived in a world which was not much different from the world before or since. It was a world of good and bad men, and men who were sometimes good and sometimes not so good. For there is no one in the world who is completely good or completely

The bleeding offering he made with a smiling face.

evil. Most people have in them a mixture of many qualities, and so it is well to remember that the people of the Mahabharata were real people with the strength and the weaknesses of real people in all parts of the world and in all ages of its history.

To continue the story, the princes of Hastina-pura returned to their city with Drona, while Ekalavya turned back quietly to the forest glades where he lived.

Thus was Arjuna's rival destroyed.

CHAPTER VIII

KARNA FACES ARJUNA

HE young princes of Hastinapura grew to be fine, strong youths. Drona and Kripa taught them the skills that all Kshatriyas had to master. They learned to ride their horses and drive their chariots, to fence and to wrestle, to draw the bow and wield the mace. They learned of the formations and movements of the infantry and cavalry during battles, and they studied the arts of defence and attack.

They learned too the code of honour of the warriors of the time: Their wise tutors taught them that a true Kshatriya is, above all, a prince in thought, word and deed; one who thinks no unworthy thought, speaks no lowly word and does no mean or cowardly deed. The princes of Hastinapura learned that a Kshatriya's place is on the battlefield where he defends his people and his country against the enemy. A Kshatriya must always be brave and fearless but never cruel. He must go to battle ready to meet death, and he may never, if he be a true Kshatriya, turn his back on the enemy or fly from danger. He must be noble and large-hearted, generous and forgiving. He must not raise his hand to hurt one who is weaker than he; he must not fight a woman or a child, or one of a lowly caste, not trained as he is trained. He must not strike a man who has fallen, nor one who is asleep; he must not, while mounted, fight one who is on foot, nor strike anyone by creeping up on him from behind. And he himself must be steadfast and loyal and true to his liege lord and his people in good times and bad.

All these things the teachers taught the Kshatriya princes and the boys proved to be apt pupils.

In course of time Drona felt that they had reached a high degree of skill and had mastered all their lessons. They were without rivals now in the whole land—Bhima and Duryodhana in the art of wielding the mace; Nakula and Sahadeva as horsemen; Drona's son, Ashvathama who had grown up with the royal princes, in the science of warfare and the planning of the formation of army divisions, the sieges of cities,

and attacks on and defence of fortresses; Yudhishthira was supreme as a chariot fighter and leader
of men. But of them all Arjuna was the very
best, for he excelled in all things. Arjuna was
his teacher's favourite pupil and his pride.

Then, a time came when, according to custom,
Drona fixed a day for a tournament, at which
his pupils could display their skill to the world.
There would be individual displays by each
prince, and matches at which they would pit
their strength against one another and against
any who challenged them.

To this tournament were invited all the people
of Hastinapura, and they came in holiday mood
and holiday clothes, jostling each other and
crowding through the public entrances to catch
a glimpse of the royal princes. Tents were
pitched and brightly coloured pennants fluttered
gaily over them in the sunshine.

Beyond, under richly embroidered canopies,
were the seats for the royal family and for
people of high rank and office who came accompanied by a great procession, and the beating
of drums and the music of pipes—first, the
blind king Dhritarashtra and then Gandhari,
his queen, and after her came ·Kunti, mother
of the Pandavas. Kunti was followed by the

noble Bhishma, and Vidura and the teachers, Drona and Kripa.

The blare of conch shells rent the air; the drums began to beat, and martial music played announcing the arrival of the princes. The crowd cheered and shouted as they came in, dressed in their shining coats of mail; Yudhishthira, the eldest leading, and following after him his brothers and cousins. The priests began to chant the beautiful Vedic hymns to the lighting of the sacrificial fire, and offerings were made to the gods.

Then the princes stood up and began to display their marvellous feats of strength and skill and cunning. As they watched, the people held their breath. For never before had been seen such strength, such grace and lightness of movement, such wonderful feats of skill, or such fine marksmanship. The twanging of bowstrings seemed to tear open the skies, and so thick was the shower of arrows that the light of the sun was shut out from the world as they flew. Yet not one arrow was needlessly shot, nor was there a single dart that did not go swiftly and surely to its target. Other feats were shown too. Duryodhana and Bhima displayed their skill with their maces. Nakula and Sahadeva, youthful though they were, exhibited their unrivalled horsemanship. Last of all came Arjuna, and at sight of him the people set up a loud roar of welcome. He bowed to his teachers and his elders and returned the greetings of the crowds before he entered the contest. When the people saw the wonders that he performed with his bow and his arrows, and the almost magical quality of his darts, when they saw his swiftness of foot and lightness of movement, and his skill and courage, they cheered him again and again and acknowledged him the greatest of them all. The widowed queen Kunti felt her heart stir with joy and pride as she watched; and the people shouted loudly: "There is no one who can equal Arjuna in this world!" But when Duryodhana heard these words he ground his teeth with jealousy. He bit his nails and wrung his hands. "If only Arjuna could be beaten!..." Duryodhana thought. "Oh, if only Arjuna could be beaten!..."

At that moment, as if in answer to his prayer, there arose from among the crowd of people, a youth dressed in shining armour and bearing arms. He strode towards the enclosure where the royal princes stood, a tall, broad-shouldered man, fair of face and keen of eye. Though he came from the common crowd, he walked boldly and stood straight, carrying himself more proudly than any prince. In his ears were a strange pair of ear-rings, which shone with such a bright, red light that his face and his eyes seemed to reflect their glow.

A hush fell upon the crowd as they watched. Under their canopies the royal personages waited and whispered to one another and to their servants inquiring the cause of the delay. Only Kunti gasped and grew pale, as she saw the strange warrior. Those ear-rings . . . That coat of mail! Did she not know them?

The newcomer entered the enclosure, and, bowing quickly before them all, he announced loudly: "I also wish to display my skill before the gathering here : . . for I can prove to the world that Arjuna's feats are as child's play to me."

Drona frowned: Who was this unknown warrior who stood among the common crowd and dared to challenge Arjuna himself? He grew uneasy as he watched the bold manner of the youth, for he showed no hesitation. Drona did not like the turn things were taking. He felt that a challenge to Arjuna was like a challenge to himself. Arjuna's defeat or humiliation would be his own defeat and humiliation. He must not let this happen. As he was thinking, however, Arjuna stepped forward. "I accept the challenge!" he said smilingly. Drona waved him aside, and went up to the stranger. Ignoring Arjuna's words, Drona said to him: "Before you enter such a contest, you must prove yourself, O stranger! You must display your skill before the assembly."

"Nothing easier!" laughed the stranger. "Shall we start?"

And so the newcomer began to display his feats and his skills to those gathered there, and in all things he did he proved himself fully their equal, and in no way inferior. As he watched, Drona's anxiety grew. The mob however cheered wildly, for here indeed was a match for Arjuna. The newcomer's dexterity was as great as the Kshatriya prince's. Indeed, the people began to observe that whatever Arjuna could do, the unknown warrior could also do, and with greater skill and ease.

All the while Queen Kunti looked on, her heart pounding in her breast, her hands cold from fear and her face as white as death. "Where, O where, will all this end?" she thought desperately.

From his place Duryodhana watched too. He saw how skilfully the unknown warrior handled his weapons, and Duryodhana knew that here was what he had waited for these many long years—a rival to Arjuna! Heaven had answered his wish. Duryodhana came quickly forward and took the stranger's hand. Then in the sight of all he embraced him warmly.

"Welcome, O Warrior," he said. "Whoever you may be, from now on you shall be as blood brother to me. Whatever you ask, I shall give you if it be in my power."

The warrior thanked Duryodhana: "I shall not forget your kindness and generosity," he answered. "I have something indeed to ask of you, O Prince, and this is it."

Then raising his voice so that everyone could hear, he said, "A duel with Arjuna is all I ask! Let me have permission to fight a duel with Arjuna."

Hearing his words, Kunti began to tremble like a leaf. But Arjuna stepped forward.

"I accept the challenge!" he said again, eagerly. "I will fight this stranger.

They stood face to face, Arjuna and his rival, in readiness for the contest. Those who were assembled there were full of wonder to see how

greatly they resembled each other, both tall
and ruddy and shining-eyed, with perfect limbs,
and clean, strong features. Only Arjuna was
younger and slighter, while the other had reached
his full manhood and was bigger built.

As they stood in this way, Kunti covered her
eyes with her hands and a wild scream escaped
her. The next moment she fainted in the arms
of her serving maid and had to be carried away.

Drona and Kripa were whispering together
anxiously; Drona was determined to avoid this
contest. Just as the two warriors drew their
swords, Kripa arose and held up his hand.
He came down to where they stood.

"Wait!" Kripa exclaimed sharply, and he
faced Karna—for it was indeed he, the eldest
son of Kunti and the Sun God. "Wait!" repeated Kripa. "Do you not know, O warrior,
that it is the custom among Kshatriyas for a
fighter to make his ancestry and his family
known to the world before he fights a duel?
Do you not know that a Kshatriya may not
cross swords with one who is of low birth?"

Kripa turned to Arjuna. "Name your family
then, O Arjuna," he said. "Tell us what race
you belong to, and who your ancestors are."

Arjuna answered in a clear loud voice; he

told the assembly the names of his royal ancestors.

Kripa turned to the other. "Stranger, what is your name? What is your family? What is the blood that runs in your veins? Proclaim these things before you cross swords with a royal Prince."

Karna looked up proudly:

"My name is Karna," he answered. "I am a warrior; I cannot claim royal blood but...."

"Then you may not fight a royal prince," Kripa interrupted triumphantly. Karna bit his lip. Kripa went on, with scorn in his voice and his eye: "Go back to the common crowd from where you have come; this is a tournament for Kshatriyas and men of royal birth!"

But even as Kripa spoke, Duryodhana stepped forward. He put his hand upon Karna's shoulder.

"Common crowd!" he cried angrily, speaking to Kripa. "Who cares about blood? Has it not always been said that a man is made noble by his deeds and not by his birth? Do not your books say this, and have you not yourself said this to us often?"

But Kripa and Drona, fearing Arjuna's defeat, hardened their hearts against him, and Drona said stubbornly, "Arjuna is a royal prince. He will not soil his hands by fighting one who is not of noble birth."

Then Duryodhana, roused to anger because his plan would be foiled, faced Drona his teacher, and said:

"Very well then—If you say Arjuna may fight only a royal prince, why, that can easily be fixed. If this stranger is not a prince, why, that can easily be set right." He raised his voice as he announced: "I, Duryodhana, prince of Hastinapura, bestow upon Karna, the kingdom of Anga. He shall be king of that beautiful land, and so shall be free to fight whomsoever he chooses." Karna knelt before Duryodhana, tears of gratitude in his eyes. Then Duryodhana placed upon his head the crown that he had quickly sent for. The priests came forward at his bidding and amid song and prayer and the hymns of coronation they anointed Karna's head and sprinkled holy water upon it, and he was crowned king of Anga.

The crowds cheered wildly now. But in the royal ranks there was silence and no one knew what to say. At that moment there arose from the crowd an old, bent man, dressed in the humble clothes of a servant. It was Adiratha, Karna's fosterfather. He tottered up to the enclosure while the crowd made way for him, and came to where Karna and Duryodhana stood. The people looked on, curious and wondering. They saw the tears run down the old man's furrowed cheeks: they heard his trembling voice cry out: "Oh my son! my son!" They saw him hold out his thin, reedy arms and running to Karna embrace him passionately. "Father!" they heard Karna cry as he knelt at his feet. The old man blessed him, and raised him up again and embraced him, weeping tears of happiness and pride.

Now the Pandavas had been watching, and when Bhima saw this scene he shouted out in a rude and sneering voice: "King of Anga, is he? Why he is only a chariot driver's son. Pooh! his blood is the blood of a chariot driver!.... A chariot driver to fight with royal princes! Does he not know that he was born to wield a whip for a measly horse, not a sword which is the weapon of a prince?"

At these cruel, ugly words, Karna stood silent, breathing hard, flushed with anger and sorrow. His arm tightened around his old father's shoulders. Tears arose in his throat, but he swallowed them back. But Duryodhana would not be silent. His eyes blazed as he answered Bhima.

"Shame upon you who call yourself a prince!" Duryodhana flung at him. "Your words are the words of one who is weak and stupid and unworthy. A true Kshatriya would not soil his mouth by uttering such unworthy words!" He looked round, but nobody spoke. Whether it was because they were unwilling to go against the Kshatriya code or whether it was because they feared Drona and respected his word, Duryodhana never knew. But at that critical moment, everybody remained silent and Duryodhana found himself alone beside the stranger. He strode up to Karna.

"Come," he said in a voice that all could hear. "Come with me. You shall be my brother, and a day will come when these insults shall be avenged. Come, let us go."

He took Karna's arm and the two went off together. The tournament came to a sudden end. The crowd broke up and men talked in excited whispers as they left.

"This is not the end of the story!" they remarked to each other. "It is only the beginning. One day Arjuna and Karna will come face to face in battle . . . and who knows what will happen then?"

CHAPTER IX

KARNA AND THE BRAHMASTRA WEAPON

HAT night while Karna slept he had a strange dream. It seemed to him that he saw a shining being descend from the sky and appear before him. He heard him call his name: "Karna! Karna!" "Who are you?" Karna asked the stranger. And the other answered: "I am your father, Karna, the Sun God!"

Karna started, "What is this you say?" he whispered huskily. "My father is Adiratha, charioteer of Hastinapura."

"No, Karna," answered the Sun God. "Adiratha is not in truth your father." And he told him the story of his birth.

"You are no humble chariot driver," he said. "Your blood is royal and noble!" Karna remained silent; a hundred conflicting thoughts were crowding in his mind.

Through their din and confusion he heard

the Sun God's warning voice begging him to keep what he had told him a secret.

"Speak about this to no one, my beloved son," he said, "for to do so would be to betray Kunti, the mother who bore you and bring her to shame." Karna promised. "It shall be as you say," he murmured, "the secret shall be locked up in my heart and no man will know."

But the Sun God had come to speak about other things. He had come to warn Karna about enemies who wished to harm him and who would try to make him weak and powerless. He told Karna how Indra, the heavenly father of Arjuna, would come to him in disguise and try to get from him his magic armour and ear-rings.

"Do not part with these, Karna," the Sun God said. "They are my gifts to you,—the Sun God's gifts; they are charms that protect you and make you invincible." Karna remained silent. "Do not part with them, Karna," the Sun God's voice repeated and it was still ringing in Karna's ears as he awoke. He looked about him. He was alone. The Sun God had disappeared. Was it really a dream? he wondered.

But that evening in the gloom of twilight an

old wrinkled man came to Karna declaring that he was a humble beggar come to seek charity. "Your fame as a generous man has spread over the world," said the old man. "And I wish to have proof of your generosity."

Karna remembered his dream, but gave no sign that he did. He only said quietly:

"Tell me what you want, and I shall not refuse it to you, for I have never refused any man anything!" Then the Brahmin asked Karna to make him a gift of the ear-rings and armour that he wore.

Karna had expected this. "They shall be yours," he answered. and, without a moment's hesitation he cut off his ear-rings and unlocked his armour and gave him both.

Hardly had he done so, when Karna saw a change come over the old man; he was transformed into a shining being, crowned with a jewelled crown and dressed in garments of silk and gold.

"I am Indra!" he said. "The king of the gods."

"Do you think I did not see through you?" thought Karna scornfully, but he said nothing.

Indra went on: "Your generosity has filled me with wonder and joy, and it shall not go unrewarded. Therefore in return for what you

Your fame as a generous man has spread over the
world.

have done for me, Karna, you may ask from me whatever gift you will and it shall be yours."

Karna answered, smiling a little.

"There is only one thing that I desire, O Indra, and that is your Brahmastra. In return for my ear-rings and my armour, O Indra, give me your Brahmastra, the weapon that never fails!" Indra was taken aback. No mortal had ever touched the Brahmastra before, for it was Indra's special weapon. He who possessed it became invincible. More than that, he could, with the Brahmastra, destroy the entire earth and all the other worlds besides. The Brahmastra was not a weapon for mortal men; Indra tried to explain this to Karna. "Ask for any other gift, Karna," Indra begged. But Karna shook his head. "If I cannot have the Brahmastra I will have nothing!" he said stubbornly. In the end Indra had to yield, for he had given his promise.

"You will have the Brahmastra," he said, "since you have set your heart on it, and since I cannot go back on my word, but you will have it to use only once. You shall destroy with it only one enemy and no more. And when that enemy has been destroyed the Brahmastra will be powerless."

Then he placed the Brahmastra weapon in Karna's hands and vanished.

Karna laughed with joy. He looked at the shining beauty of the weapon and cried out: "With this weapon of Indra shall Arjuna be destroyed!"

For Karna knew that the day would come when the Kauravas and Pandavas would meet in a great war, when, once and for all, their bitter feuds would be settled. He knew that Arjuna was his special enemy. The other Pandavas were as nothing to him. His heart longed for a duel with Arjuna, the greatest warrior in the land. His one desire was Arjuna's defeat. To this end all his thoughts and actions were directed. For this reason Karna, disregarding the Sun God's advice, had parted with his ear-rings and his coat of mail, so that he might bargain for the unfailing Brahmastra. And now he had it and it was his to use. True he could use it only once. A second chance would not be given him. But what of that? Karna's heart leaped when he thought of the time when he would use it.

But first he must perfect himself in the entire field of archery and find a Guru as great as Drona.

Karna and the Brahmastra Weapon

Karna knew that there was only one person in whole world who could equal Drona and that was Parashurama. Indeed, it was said that Drona himself had been Parashurama's pupil. But Karna knew also that Parashurama, who was a Brahmin, hated all Kshatriyas and would have nothing to do with them. He thought over the matter and in the end he went to Parashurama's hermitage disguised as a Brahmin. The unsuspecting Parashurama received Karna and agreed to be his teacher, and Karna lived undiscovered for several years in his hermitage. He served the fiery-tempered sage as the pupils of those days were expected to do, and Parashurama gave him instruction in return.

During all that time Karna guarded his secret well and no man knew him for a Kshatriya.

The day came at last when Karna, having mastered the secret mantra, reached the end of his long course of study. But on that fateful day, Parashurama discovered Karna's secret.

It happened this way:

Parashurama was sleeping that afternoon, his head resting upon Karna's lap, when an insect settled upon Karna's thigh and stung him. Not wishing to disturb the master, Karna remained still and unmoving in spite of the pain. The insect which was the kind that bored the trunk of trees to make its nest, continued to sting him until it had bored a hole in his flesh. The blood began to flow, but Karna sat on without wincing, for he had been taught that it is wrong to disturb a sleeping man, especially a teacher. Karna allowed the blood to flow and the insect continued to bore into his flesh. At last the teacher woke up from his sleep and sat up. Parashurama saw the blood flowing down Karna's thigh. It had made a little pool on the ground. Greatly concerned, Parashurama asked his pupil what had happened. When he discovered how the insect had bored into the youth's flesh, Parashurama was aghast. He questioned him about it, and Karna respectfully explained to him how, not wishing to disturb him, he had made no movement. Parashurama stared at him in amazement. Then slowly a look of knowing came into his eyes. He continued to scrutinize the young man who stood before him. He was thinking: "Only a Kshatriya can bear pain as this youth has borne it, without murmuring. For the Kshatriyas are trained from childhood to endure pain without murmuring. This youth can never be a Brahmin! He must be a Kshatriya!"

Suddenly he pointed a finger at Karna:

"You have tricked me!" he shouted, his eyes blazing with anger. "You have deceived me! You are a Kshatriya and you have come to me in the guise of a Brahmin and tried to wrest my knowledge from me under false pretences! Go from here before I reduce you to ashes in my anger."

Karna hung his head. He had spent long years in patient and painstaking study. He had undergone many hardships and humiliations to learn the secret, and he had come at last to the end of his long and arduous course, and now he had betrayed himself. He knew Parashurama would never forgive him. He stood before his teacher, humble and speechless, as Parashurama's voice, shrill with anger, fell upon his ears:

"A curse be on you, false one!" the old man shrieked, "May the instruction you have received here under false pretences be lost upon you. May all your efforts fail!"

Karna turned pale, as he saw how his hopes came crashing down about him. A man of truth, he had been caught in an act of falsehood. Karna fell at the teacher's feet, begging forgiveness, and when Parashurama saw how he repented he felt sorry for his pupil. His curse was upon the unhappy youth's head and yet

Parashurama softened it a little. "Go from here, O Karna," he said. "You have learnt much and been a good pupil. The knowledge you have received will be lost indeed, but only in that critical hour when you will need it the most!"

Karna arose, heavy-hearted. Then with a last gesture of reverence and farewell he turned sadly away to go. The teacher's voice seemed to ring in his ears. Ill-luck seemed to dog his footsteps. Fate seemed to be against him, everywhere and in all things. Then he felt the shining weapon of Indra in his hands and his spirits rose

"Arjuna!" he thought gazing at the Brahmastra. "Here lies your destruction, here in my hands."

CHAPTER X

DURYODHANA PLOTS AGAIN!

HE happenings on the day of the tournament were only like another straw in the wind, which showed which way it was blowing. For during the years of their childhood and youth the Kauravas never ceased to hate their cousins. Duryodhana brooded constantly. Anything that went well for the Pandavas was, as far as he was concerned, something evil. He hated to see his cousins happy and well-fed. He hated to hear them praised. When people loved them he was tormented by jealousy. And Bhima did not make matters any better with his rude, uncouth ways, his loud, bantering laughter, and his sneering, outspoken words. Duryodhana never forgave Bhima for what had happened upon the day of the tournament. Besides, he also feared greatly the growing strength of the Pandavas, and their popularity with the people. During this time Duryodhana found himself surrounded by many evil advisers. Small-minded, wicked men, watching Duryodhana's discontent, saw an opportunity to raise themselves in the royal favour. They came to him pretending to be his friends and encouraged him in his wicked thoughts. Duryodhana took these people for his friends because they flattered him and spoke as he wished them to speak, while he rejected the wise advice of men like Bhishma and Drona who were frank and who did not hesitate to point out his faults to him.

As for his parents,—especially his father, the blind Dhritarashtra,—they were good people, but they loved their son with a foolish, doting love, and could not bear to deny him anything. That was how he had grown into a headstrong boy, and now he would take no advice from anyone except when it agreed with what he himself wanted to do. Besides, Dhritarashtra himself was uneasy about the growing strength of his nephews.

Duryodhana's false friends came to him and whispered that his cousins were surely not immortal. They hinted that their death could surely be brought about if one was patient and cunning! They spoke of ways of how enemies could be done away with if they became inconvenient, and Duryodhana, listening carefully, was heartened. Presently, he and his friends put their heads together and plotted a dark and evil deed.

But all this while the Pandavas were not sleeping. They too were vigilant. Their spies went about the palace too, and mingled with many people and kept their eyes and ears open, but gave no sign that they saw or heard anything. Thus the Pandavas came to know that another plot was hatching, a deeper one this time, one more carefully laid and intended to catch at one stroke the five of them as well as their widowed mother. And so, one day when Duryodhana came up to them beaming and smiling, to tell them of a festival which was to take place at Varnavata and which they must attend, the Pandavas were not without their own misgivings. But they gave no sign of this to him. The people of Varnavata loved them, Duryodhana said. They waited to welcome them in their city. He himself had given orders that a most beautiful and wonderful palace was to be built for them to live in. "See for yourselves," he added, and he brought them before Dhritarashtra, the king, who in turn urged them to go.

When they were alone the Pandavas discussed the matter among themselves and with Vidura, their uncle. They knew very well that Duryodhana's motives could not be honest, but they knew too that it would be more dangerous to remain than to go. In the end they decided to leave. But they watched and listened carefully, and on the day before their departure Vidura came to them with important information. He had discovered Duryodhana's evil plot. In low whispers and using many secret code words, he told them of how the palace of pleasure that Duryodhana had built for them at Varnavata was in fact the palace of Death. For it was made of wax and within its walls and in many secret places the builders had, under Duryodhana's orders, concealed such materials as would easily catch fire. Duryodhana's plot was to trap them inside a burning house. One day the palace would catch fire, and no one would know that it was not accidental! The Pandavas would be sleeping inside, and they would be trapped.

Vidura begged his nephews not to panic: "Be brave and calm above all," he said. "Give no sign that you know. Only wait and watch every minute of the day and night." He went

on to tell them too, of how his own workmen
had mingled unnoticed with Duryodhana's and
noted down every detail of the palace of wax.
They were building a secret underground passage
which would lead out of that terrible palace
into the forest outside. Vidura told the Pandavas
that they must watch for the day when this
passage would be completed, for it would be
their means of escape. He said that he had also
employed a skilled miner who would give them
the password and warn them.

So the Pandavas went to Varnavata and when
they reached there they found that Vidura had
spoken the truth. For as they walked about the
palace they saw that it was so planned that
there was no means of escape from it if its wax
and straw-filled walls caught fire. Then in their
hearts they thanked their good uncle and
blessed him, remembering how already, even
at this very moment, by his orders, the underground passage was being dug.

Bearing in mind Vidura's warning, the
Pandavas spent their days and nights watching
and making plans for their escape from that
closely guarded palace of death. Outside Varana-
vata was a deep dark forest through which
flowed the river Ganga. Beyond the river the

country was even more thickly forested. Few people had set their feet in this land.

The five Pandava Princes rode every day through the forest, and secretly acquainted themselves with all the paths and tracks. They also saw with satisfaction that Vidura's workmen had cut the subterranean passage, working from the depth of the forest and digging through the earth until they reached the rooms of the palace.

CHAPTER XI

THE PANDAVAS ESCAPE

OR a whole year the Pandavas lived in Varnavata while Duryodhana waited and watched. He was in no hurry to carry out his wicked scheme; this time he wanted no hitch. Moreover he wished to lull all suspicion and make it appear to the world as if he had nothing to do with the ghastly plot.

The Pandavas waited too and watched, and secretly from time to time, Vidura sent them word about the happenings in the royal court. "You must fly," Vidura's messengers warned them, "for Duryodhana hates you, and will try every means to destroy you if you return. You must fly and hide yourselves until your evil days have passed. Take refuge in the forest. Disguise yourselves. Let Duryodhana think you are dead."

Then one day word reached Yudhishthira and his brothers that on a certain night, the palace of wax would be set on fire. Thereupon the Pandavas set to work to complete their own plans for escape. That night Kunti Devi prepared a great feast, and invited all the inmates of the palace to share it. But the Pandavas had seen to it that the food and the wine were drugged, so that the guards and the servants who surrounded the palace, having eaten and drunk, fell into a heavy stupor. And they did not wake as the Pandavas moved stealthily among them, or as they crept out softly, one by one, and went down the narrow steps of the underground passage. When they were at a safe distance from the palace, they gave the signal to their friends who were waiting outside and who instantly set fire to the palace, as had been planned. Duryodhana's wicked plot was thus forestalled.[1] The great palace went up in flames; the citizens gathered at the scene and hurried about trying to put out the fire, but the flames only rose higher and higher, and within a few hours the palace was reduced to a heap of ashes. Morning came and the citizens of Varnavata looked at the destruction, and searching among the ruins found many charred[2] bodies. They were the bodies of

---

[1] Be beforehand with.
[2] Burnt black.

Duryodhana's servants, but few knew this, and the people of Varnavata wept for the Pandavas, believing them to be dead.

But when word reached Hastinapura of the fire and when Duryodhana heard how charred bodies had been found, his wicked heart rejoiced, though outwardly he made a great show of grief and of mourning for his cousins. In the palace there were many who wept sincerely for the Pandavas, and Duryodhana mingled his false tears with theirs as they performed the funeral rites.

Meanwhile the Pandavas and their mother fled, going quickly through the underground passage, and at dead of night emerging at its other end, into the fearful forest. It was pitch dark, and the weird tree-shapes seemed like demons. The creatures of the night chirped and screeched around them. Wild animals roared. Kunti trembled with fear. Her sons consoled her with loving words, and cheered her up as well as they could. But there was little time to waste. They must hurry on or they might be discovered.

So they set out upon that desolate and frightful journey, and walked without resting for long, weary hours until at last they reached the river

So they set upon that desolate and frightful journey.

Ganga, which they crossed in a boat that the kindly and ever watchful Vidura had sent for them.

On the other side of the river was a strange country, a dark forest region that no man had set foot in before. There were no tracks, and the silence was broken only by the screeching of forest creatures. Overhead the branches of the trees were so thick that the sun's light could scarcely pierce through. The ground was marshy and infested with deadly creatures, swarms of ants, mosquitoes and poisonous snakes. The Pandavas walked through this wild country. Their feet grew tired and many a time Kunti dropped with fatigue. But they dared not stop for fear they might be detected.

Bhima, the strongest of them all, went ahead, and broke the branches to make way for the rest. He searched through the forest to find them food and water. Often he lifted his frail mother in his arms and carried her when she was too tired to go on. Indeed, so great was Bhima's strength that he sometimes even carried all the five of them together through the forest.

As they journeyed they had many strange adventures. One day Bhima, walking through the forest in search of water for his thirsting family, came upon a beautiful young woman beside a pool. Now this woman was really a demon queen, Hidimbi, who lived with her brother Hidimba in the forest. Unnoticed by the Pandavas, Hidimbi had seen them as they wandered over the forest, and she had fallen in love with Bhima. But she knew Bhima would never love her in her hideous demon form, and so, with the aid of magic, she had transformed herself into a woman of great beauty. Hidimbi came to Bhima, confessed her love and begged him to take her as his wife. Bhima, seeing her loveliness, was greatly pleased. But before he could marry her he had to fight her brother, who was very angry that his sister had chosen a human creature for husband. There was a terrible duel between the two, in which Bhima vanquished Hidimbi's brother and killed him.

Then Bhima married Hidimbi and returned to his mother and brothers with his new-won bride. And if they were somewhat startled to see her hideous demon form, (for she could not live under magic all the time) they politely refrained from saying anything that might hurt her feelings or those of the happy bridegroom. Besides she proved a valuable friend to them, for she knew the forest as well as she knew the palm of her big rough hand, and she led them through short-cuts and over tracks that forest animals had made. She brought them food, attended to their needs, and stood on guard while they slept. So strong was this good demon wife of Bhima that she sometimes cheerfully carried them upon her big, powerful shoulders. She talked to them in her gruff voice and told them stories to amuse them, until they grew to like her very much indeed, and forgot her rather unfortunate looks. As for Bhima, he loved her very much while she was with them, and was full of joy when he heard that soon she would bear him a child. But once he left the forest, he almost forgot all about her and did not remember either her or the son that was born to her, for many years afterwards. For she would not go with them into the city of Ekachakrapura which they reached at last.

She could not leave the forest which was her home and her kingdom, and where she had lived all her life, she told them. She tried to persuade Bhima to stay with her in the forest and be king there, but Bhima would not leave his brothers and his mother. So the husband and the wife said good-bye to each other, and she went back to her forest home where, some time later, she bore Bhima's child, the valiant Ghatotkacha; and Bhima went with Kunti and his brothers into the city of Ekachakrapura.

CHAPTER XII

A SILENT CITY AND A DEMON KING

HE Pandava princes and their mother, walking through the streets of Ekachakrapura, noticed a strange thing about the city: a heavy gloom hung like a cloud over it. There were no sounds of singing and dancing and laughter, and the people walked heavily as if bowed down with some great care. It was a silent city, and each man and woman seemed to carry in his heart a great sorrow.

The Pandavas moved among them unrecognised, until they reached at last the house of a poor potter who offered them a room to stay in. They took up their quarters with him and his family, and here they lived for several months.

One day, Kunti Devi heard a great noise of weeping and wailing from the potter's quarter of the house. Hurrying to see what the matter was, she had a hard time persuading them to talk calmly and tell her the reason for their

111

sorrow. But at last the potter and his wife sobbed out their story. They told her that the city of Ekachakrapura was under the sway of a demon named Bakasura who had come from the forest one day, and had gone about the city, looting and pillaging, killing people and devouring them, until the King of Ekachakrapura and all his ministers had fled, leaving the citizens to defend themselves as best they could. Then at last the fear-stricken citizens had come to Bakasura in a body and made a truce with him. They had agreed to send him every day a fixed quantity of food in a bullock cart if he would stop his mischievous activity. With the food would be sent to him also a citizen from Ekachakrapura. This citizen, together with the rice and bullocks, were to be Baka's food, and the empty cart would be brought back after he had eaten, so that it could take his meal to him the next day. As the potter related these things, his family listened to him with mournful faces. But at this point they began to sob aloud again.

"Today it is the turn of my family," concluded the potter, "and we weep because of this, for one of us must go—and leave the rest in mourning. There is no one who can help us, good mother; did we not say so from the beginning?"

Kunti slipped away and returned to her room. In the evening when her sons came home, she related to them the story she had heard, and told them how the shadow of death was falling now upon this little house where they lived. When Bhima heard the story he resolved to go and meet the monster Baka in place of the potter. He was sure he could fight him and make an end of him.

At first the brothers were reluctant to let Bhima go, for they feared that they would be discovered and that Duryodhana would come to know of their whereabouts. But after a while they agreed that Bhima should fight the tyrant of Ekachakrapura. "Are we not Kshatriyas? Is it not our duty to protect the defenceless?" they argued among themselves.

The potter and his family were overwhelmed when they heard that Bhima offered to go to Bakasura. "How shall we ever show you our gratitude?" they cried.

"By silence!" said the Pandavas gravely. "Speak no word about it to anyone, and thus we shall know that you are grateful." The Pandavas had no wish to be discovered before the time was ripe.

The next morning Bhima drove the bullock cart, with its vast quantity of food and reached the cave outside the city, where the Rakshasa Bakasura lived. He was very hungry after his long ride and, without further ceremony, fell to eating the food that was meant for Bakasura. As he ate he called out in his great bellowing voice, "Baka, evil one, devourer of human flesh, where are you? Come out and show yourself! Your food is here."

At this, a tremendous roar was heard from that fearful dark cavern. "Who dares to call me by name?" cried Baka. "I do," laughed Bhima, "come and see me yourself. But, of course, you may take your time, for in the meanwhile I will finish your dinner for you. It is uncommonly good, and I am hungry."

"Dinner? Dinner?" bellowed the demon in a fearful rage. "Who are you, fool, that speaks to me in such words?" He had never been spoken to in that way before, and he was as surprised as he was angry.

"Come and see for yourself, I repeat," Bhima roared back. "I am only a poor human being sent to be served up for your dinner today."

A fearful cry followed Bhima's words. The next minute the earth shook, as the fiery-eyed monster emerged, from out of the cave.

Baka was by no means handsome. He was a great, ugly creature with reeking breath and blood-shot eyes, towering above the trees. His face and body were covered with coarse red hair, and sharp long fangs like those of an animal hung out of his mouth in a fearful grin. The earth seemed to shake as he walked. Bhima looked at the ugly monster from where he sat, and then he calmly went on eating. He scooped out a great handful of rice and then with his mouth full, he began to speak again. "Will you wait till I finish dinner? It is hardly fair to disturb a man while he is eating."

For a second, Baka gaped at him in wide-eyed surprise. Then with a fearful howl, he charged at Bhima, head foremost. He began to rain blows upon Bhima's back while he ate.

"Ah!" said Bhima at each blow, "that feels good; it makes the food go down better!" And he went on eating with great relish. Then he washed down the food with a great goblet of wine, and when the meal was ended he burped aloud, to show his appreciation and satisfaction. "That was quite a good meal," said Bhima as he wiped his mouth with the back of his great hand, while Baka rushed about, up and down

115

and round and round, working himself into a great rage, uprooting trees and breaking down branches with which to fight Bhima.

"Come now, Baka! I am ready. Shall we fight?" Bhima roared out. For answer Baka threw at Bhima a great big tree he had in his hand. Bhima brushed it away, as he would have done a troublesome insect.

"Oh, surely not this children's game, Baka!" he smiled. "You will not refuse me a hand-to-hand fight?" Baka did not answer. He continued to hurl trees at him. Then suddenly he changed his tactics, as he came charging at Bhima like an angry bull. Bhima saw him and stood in readiness for him. With a blow of his hand he sent the Rakshasa reeling far from him. Baka arose howling with rage and pain, and the two went at each other again and fought and wrestled until the earth shook. They fought many rounds, but at the end of each one Bhima threw Baka upon the earth. He rose up again and again, growing angrier each time like a mad bull, and returned to the fight until at length, Bhima caught him and broke his back across his mighty knee. The frightful demon died in that moment, and lay still at last upon the blood-soaked earth.

Then Bhima, a little dazed but otherwise not

much the worse for his adventure, returned to
Ekachakrapura to the potter's home, where all
the family had gathered to welcome him. They
garlanded him and adorned his forehead with
vermilion powder and flashed the *arati*[1] lights
before his face.

They were deeply grateful, but Bhima only
warned them to keep the incident a secret.
"That is all you can do for us in return," he
said, as he retired to his lodgings with his
brothers. The potter gave him his word.

[1] Little wick lamps flourished before the face for good luck.

CHAPTER XIII

THE PANDAVAS WIN DRAUPADI

LL through the days that they were away, the Pandavas kept in touch with happenings at Hastina-pura. Faithful friends came secretly from time to time to visit them and to inform them of events at the royal court and in the country.

That was how, soon after the slaying of Bakasura, news reached them that King Drupada of the Panchala country (whom Arjuna had once captured in battle) was inviting the princes of the land to the Swayamvara of his daughter, the Princess Draupadi. A Swayamvara was a ceremony at which a girl was allowed to choose from a gathering of suitors the one she wished to have for a husband. King Drupada had, however, proposed instead a contest in which the princes of the land would take part; and whoever succeeded in the feat of arms that was to be the test, would win Draupadi for his bride. When the Pandavas heard the news they knew that the time was ripe now to reveal themselves. They decided to travel to Kampilya, Drupada's capital, and take part in the contest. So they said good-bye to the kind potter and his family, and, disguising themselves as poor Brahmins, they set out on their journey with their mother. On their way they met other Brahmins bound for the same destination. The Pandavas joined them and arrived after several days in Kampilya, where they went to live in a humble quarter of the city.

The city of Kampilya was gay with the preparations for the royal marriage, the streets festooned with flowers and leaves by day, and illuminated with thousands of little wick lamps by night. In the bazaars, trade was lively and brisk because thousands of visitors had thronged the city to be present at the royal Swayamvara. Everywhere there was talk of the contest in which the greatest warriors in the land would take part. The festivities would continue for sixteen days. In Drupada's palace his royal guests were entertained to rich, rare food and wines, to song and dance and drama and athletic shows, puppetry and shadow plays and games and hunting parties. For Draupadi was the King's only daughter, and he loved her so much that he would spare nothing for her happiness. In his heart, Drupada still secretly hoped that perhaps Arjuna was not dead after all and would come to the Swayamvara and win the royal princess, his daughter.

In the meanwhile, great and powerful princes and chieftains from all over the country came to Kampilya and stayed with the King as his guests. Draupada knew why this was so. Beautiful as she was, he knew that it was not Draupadi's beauty alone that brought the princes here to compete for her hand. He was aware that the kings who had assembled there had come to win his friendship and support, and to strengthen themselves by an alliance with him. For Drupada was strong and powerful, and Panchala at the time was a force to be reckoned with.

The sixteenth day was the day of the Swayamvara. Drupada had set for his royal guests no easy or mean task. He had arranged, high above a pool of water, a set of revolving wheels, declaring that the winner would be the one who could shoot five darts, one after another, through the exact centre of the wheels into the eye of a fish that had been placed beyond it. The contestant could not look directly at his target; he was to shoot looking at the reflection of the fish's

eye through the wheels in the water of the pool
below. All the princes of the land came forward,
wishing to enter the contest; Duryodhana himself was there and his friend Karna, king of
Anga, and Jarasandha, the king of Kasi, and
Krishna with his brother Balarama, king of the
Vrishnis, Shishupala and Shalya and many
others. But nobody knew the Pandavas as they
stood disguised as humble Brahmins, chanting
hymns and collecting alms in their begging
bowls.

At the auspicious hour, the royal elephant
carrying the dark princess was led in by Draupadi's
twin brother, Dhrishtadyumna, who held in
his hand the garland that was to be placed on
the winner's neck that day. All who were assembled there saw with wonder the beauty of
the princess. For she was dark as a rain cloud
and her skin was clear and smooth. Under thick
brooding lashes her large black eyes shone like
twin stars. Her mouth was full and proud. And
though, as was right in those days for an un-
married girl, she lowered her gaze before the
people, there was pride in her noble bearing
and a queenly dignity about her, in spite of her
tender years. Then Dhrishtadyumna led the
elephant round the enclosure where the royal

guests sat, and called out each man's name to the Princess and the name of the kingdom over which he ruled, and the name too of his family and clan. As she passed before them in all her youthful beauty, each prince felt his heart beat faster, and each vowed to himself to win her that day for his bride. But when they went to shoot, one after the other, the warriors failed in the task that Drupada had set them, and returned crestfallen and ashamed to their places—even Duryodhana and Shishupala and Jarasandha, who were all among the most famous warriors of the day. Then Karna, king of Anga and friend of Duryodhana, got up from where he sat. As he walked up and took up the bow, five humble Brahmins held their breath and looked at each other with anxious eyes, while the assembled kings waited tensely in their seats. They felt that now the contest would surely end, for as an archer Karna was considered second to none. Karna drew the mighty bow; but as his dart was about to fly, the voice of the Princess Draupadi rang out and broke the silence.

"Wait!" she commanded sharply. They waited, and Draupadi went on: "I will not wed a charioteer's son, I who am a royal princess—I will not have a low caste man contesting for my hand!" Her voice rang with scorn as she pronounced the word "Charioteer". Karna stopped as if he had been struck and put down the bow. The arrow slipped from his fingers and fell upon the floor. He retired to his seat, deeply hurt, saying not a word. Karna had been cheated out of his chance once more. Once again, just at the moment when it seemed that he would succeed, luck had slipped from him!

Now when all the Kshatriyas had tried their hand and failed, there stepped into the arena a Brahmin youth seeking permission to make the attempt.

He was tall and handsome and even in his humble attire he held himself proud as any Kshatriya and walked like a prince. The princess saw him as she sat on the elephant and she held her breath. The youth was Arjuna, but no one knew him in his lowly dress. He came forward and asked for permission to enter the contest and Drupada, after a moment's hesitation, gave it.

The proud Kshatriya princes moved uneasily in their seats; they did not like to be challenged by a Brahmin in rags. Many among them grew sullen and murmured that Drupada should not have allowed such irregularities. "These contests are for Kshatriyas, and people of royal blood," they said. But Arjuna, as he stood in the arena, noticed nothing. He drew the great bow and took careful aim—and the darts he sent flew like lightning through the revolving circles and struck the fish in the centre of the eye. As it did so, Arjuna heard the joyful applause break over his head. And yet there were some who did not join in the general acclamation. For on their golden thrones, many of the princes began to murmur to each other saying, "What kind of Swayamvara is this, where a beggar is allowed to stand beside a prince and compete? Drupada seems to have invited us only to shame us. Shall we not punish him for bringing disgrace on us?" They looked on with displeasure as the princess descended from the elephant and, led by her brother, stepped forward with the garland and slipped it around the winner's neck.

The next minute loud angry voices filled the air! "Who is this imposter? This Brahmin cub? By what right does a Brahmin compete with warriors? Drupada, you have played foul! We have been humiliated! We have been disgraced!" Arjuna saw the Kshatriya princes, their faces dark with anger, approach Drupada, shaking their fists at him and brandishing their weapons.

He drew his great bow and took careful aim.

Drupada fell back before their numbers, but in that very instant, Arjuna rushed to his aid. Then Bhima also came, armed with a great tree that he had uprooted, and Dhrishtadyumna joined them and the three of them protected Drupada from the anger of the princes. Everybody who had assembled there stood amazed at the great feats of the Brahmins for there was no one that equalled them there except Karna. But even Karna reeled back that day before the swiftness of Arjuna's darts and the deadliness of his aim. It was not long before the princes called a truce, for they found that the so-called Brahmins were not to be trifled with.

In the meanwhile Yudhishthira, with Nakula and Sahadeva, fearing they would be recognised, had slipped quickly away and gone home. The fighting over, many princes also left in a huff. But some of the guests stayed on to witness the swift marriage ceremony that was performed and to eat the dinner that followed. One of these was Krishna, king of the Vrishnis. Now Krishna watched everything keenly and he guessed that things were not what they seemed. He smiled a little as he whispered to his brother Balarama: "There is more to this drama than meets the eye, my brother!"

"Why do you say so?" asked Balarama, and Krishna answered smiling his twinkling smile. "Because these Brahmin brothers we have seen today are not Brahmins at all. Do you think that those arrows were the arrows of peaceable gentle-hearted scholars?"

"Who then do you think the young men are?" Balarama persisted, and Krishna whispered in his ears. "That one is Arjuna, the Pandava prince, and no other." He then pointed to Bhima, and said, "And that mighty one there is Bhima."

"But the Pandavas are dead," exclaimed Balarama in astonishment. "Did they not die in the burning house at Varnavata many months ago? Men said it was Duryodhana's plan!"

Krishna's eyes twinkled. "My brother," he said, "you mark my words! These men are the Pandavas. Do not ask why or how. Wait and see. The drama is only about to begin!" Then he put his forefinger upon his lip and would not say another word. At the end of the festivities Arjuna and Bhima left the assembly quietly with the princess Draupadi, declining the escort that Drupada offered them. But Drupada, suspecting also that things were not all that they seemed, and anxious too to know about the family his daughter had been wedded into, sent his son Dhrishtadyumna secretly behind them to watch all that had happened, and to return and inform him.

Dhrishtadyumna followed them without their knowledge and saw them stand before the threshold of a lowly house and call out, "Mother, see what alms we have got today." From inside the house a woman's voice came in answer, "My sons, share whatever you have equally among all the five of you." At that they gasped and cried out, startled, "Oh, mother, what is this you have commanded us to do?"

Then Dhrishtadyumna saw a gentle-faced grey-haired woman come out to greet them. "We have won a bride and you have asked us to share her among ourselves!" said her sons in dismay, as she clasped the princess to her and drew her inside.

Then Dhrishtadyumna hid himself in a place where he could hear and see everything without being seen. He observed how the five sons, in obedience to their mother's word took Draupadi, his sister, for their joint wife. And from where he lay crouched down, he heard them talk till far into the night and describe and discuss the happenings of the evening. Such was their talk

and so full was it of soldiers' expressions and
knowledge of weapons and of war, that Dhrishtadyumna knew that these men who had won his
sister were not meek and saintly Brahmins as
everyone had supposed them to be, but warriors
and princes. The knowledge filled him with joy.
When he returned to the palace and reported
these things to the father, Drupada too was
happy, for it was clear to him now that these
unknown mysterious brothers could be no other
than the Pandava princes.

CHAPTER XIV

THE PANDAVAS RETURN TO HASTINAPURA

RUPADA speedily sent messengers with Dhrishtadyumna to welcome the Pandavas and bring them to his royal palace, where he celebrated the marriage of his daughter to all five of them. They stayed with him at his court, and while they were there they met other kings who had come at Drupada's invitation to the wedding. Among these was Krishna of Dwaraka. When Yudhishthira came before Krishna and spoke to him, he realized that here was one who, because of his wisdom, was more than all the kings in the world, and in his heart he worshipped Krishna, and loved and honoured him. Ever afterwards Yudhishthira and his brothers put all their hope and trust in Krishna, and to the end of their days he remained their wise counsellor and their greatest friend.

The Pandavas found themselves now surrounded by powerful and wise allies, and their strength was further increased by the gifts and land and wealth that Drupada made to his daughter, their bride. The news of their joint marriage to Draupadi and of the alliance that had been formed with Krishna and with Drupada spread as if on wings. It was not long before it reached the royal court of Hastinapura. Duryodhana, as you may expect, was livid with rage when he heard it.

"O miserable fate!" cried Duryodhana, weeping angry tears, "What is the use of living now? For the Pandavas live also, and this knowledge poisons for me the very air I breathe." He would not eat or play or take pleasure in anything. His friend Karna sat by him. But he was not much happier than Duryodhana, for Karna had no love for the Pandavas either. Indeed the remembrance of Draupadi's scornful eyes and words, and of his humiliation in public only a few days ago, rankled[1] in his mind.

"We must destroy the Pandavas," Duryodhana moaned. "How shall we do it? . . . We must seek some way by which they will quarrel among themselves and destroy one another. United as they are, they will destroy us!"

[1] Caused pain.

Karna shook his head. He did not think it possible that the five brothers would ever quarrel. They loved each other too well for that. Besides they were shrewd men and had grown wise to the ways of the world. They knew Duryodhana and they did not trust him.

"Let us bribe Drupada!" Duryodhana suggested. "Let us make him our friend. Let us seek to break this alliance they have made."

"Sooner try to break the hand of fate!" Karna laughed without mirth.[1] These are childish schemes, friend Duryodhana. The Pandavas will never be taken in by these tricks."

"What other course is left to us then, Karna?" cried Duryodhana wringing his hands, and Karna answered, like the warrior he was, "Fight them face to face. Meet them in battle and overcome them or die in the attempt. That is the best way, and it is a Kshatriya's way."

But when Duryodhana went before Bhishma and Drona and Vidura with this suggestion, the elders advised him differently. "Are you mad, O Duryodhana, that you wish to bring about the destruction of your cousins? Do you not see that by following this path you will in the end go to your own destruction? Your thoughts are

[1] Joy, merriment.

neither good nor wise. Already the people of the
kingdom blame you and murmur against you,
suspecting that the fire in Varnavata was your
doing. Already they wait to welcome the
Pandavas into the capital. Their anger will turn
against you if you try to harm your cousins."

"What do you wish me to do then?" Duryodhana exclaimed bitterly, hating them in his heart,
yet knowing he could not go against their advice.

"Send them an escort to the court of Drupada
and welcome your cousins home again," Drona
advised him. "Make friends with them again
and do what is right and just by them. Make
amends for the wrongs they have suffered at
your hands."

It was a bitter pill for Duryodhana to swallow.
But he dared not go against their words. He was
furious and he made no secret of his feelings.
But he finally agreed to send to Kampilya for
the Pandavas. Vidura was chosen to go with
messengers to invite the Pandavas, and Vidura
went gladly, happy that the Pandavas would at
last receive their due.

But when he came to Drupada's court,
Drupada would not easily send away his sons-in-
law. For he feared this was still another ruse[1]

[1] Trick.

of Duryodhana's to destroy them. He laid down many conditions that Duryodhana must fulfil before they returned. It was only when Vidura assured him that Duryodhana would be bound this time by what he had promised, and Krishna himself declared that it would be wise for them to go, that Drupada gave his consent.

So the Pandavas returned once more to Hastinapura with Vidura, bringing with them the lovely dark princess who was their bride. Once again the citizens of Hastinapura poured out into the streets to welcome them joyfully.

All the world was happy at the Pandavas' return, except for Duryodhana and his friends.

CHAPTER XV

THE PANDAVAS BUILD INDRAPRASTHA
AND EXTEND THEIR EMPIRE

HE elders of the court of Dhrita-rashtra advised the blind old king to make peace with the Pandavas and to give them what rightly belonged to them. So, when the five brothers came before them, Dhritarashtra welcomed them and congratulated them upon their escape from the burning house and upon their marriage to the Panchala princess, Draupadi. Then he gave them a small tract of land, which was called Khandavaprastha, some distance away from Hastinapura. It was a barren place, desolate and uninhabited. By day the land lay dusty and dry under the burning sun, and at night jackals came out of their lairs and their weird howling filled the silence. People said that this land was the resting place of demons and ghosts, and avoided it for fear that they would come to some harm. This was the land that Dhritarashtra presented to his nephews.

They received his gift without complaining. In his heart Dhritarashtra hoped that it would be the last he would see of the Pandavas.

He was secretly pleased that Yudhishthira did not complain about the injustice of their treatment, and Dhritarashtra congratulated himself upon the success of his little plan. He thought it would get the Pandavas away out of sight and out of harm's way. He thought the Pandavas in their simplicity and youth had not realised how poor and barren and small their little tract of land was.

The Pandava princes with their mother and a few faithful followers set out for their new home. They well knew the difficulties they would encounter. They had not been deceived as Dhritarashtra had thought. But they had stout hearts and great faith, and they wished at all costs to avoid a quarrel with their cousins.

When they reached their destination, they set to work to plan and organise the construction of the city that was to be their capital. Yudhishthira spared himself neither trouble nor money for this great work: he sent for the master town-builders and architects of the time, and consulted them. Presently news of the great venture spread, and more people began to pour in seeking work—engineers and sculptors and carvers of stone and wood and metal; painters and landscape gardeners, as well as thousands of humble people, such as masons and bricklayers, carpenters and smiths, weavers of cloth and tradesmen selling all sorts of things. What once was a silent, lonely desert, the haunt of jackals and wild beasts, now became the scene of busy human activity. A city grew: a beautiful and noble city, set amid green parks and wooded gardens. People quickly settled down there and set up trades which grew and prospered. Others cultivated the land that lay outside the city. Kind weather favoured them, and with hard work they found that the soil was not as poor as it had seemed to be. They gathered in good harvests and took them to the capital. Yudhishthira had ordered that they should be sold there at fair and honest prices.

Indeed Yudhishthira, young though he was, and without experience, showed himself to be a very capable and energetic ruler, devoted to the welfare of his subjects. He set up a wise administration, appointing honest and efficient ministers and together they made the laws of the land. So just and wise were these laws that men saw no reason to break them. Yudhishthira's kingdom therefore became known for the honest and law-abiding nature of its people.

The visitors who came to Yudhishthira's kingdom marvelled at his energy and went back, full of stories of the wonderful new city, Indraprastha. For that was the name Yudhishthira gave to his capital.

As years went by, more and more people from the surrounding areas began to acknowledge Yudhishthira as their sovereign, so that tribute poured in in return for his friendship and protection. And always Drupada, the king of Panchala and Krishna of Dwaraka remained his trusted friends and advisers. He sent his brothers to the four corners of the country and with their help his empire and influence grew. Wealth began to pour into the coffers of Indraprashtha and Yudhishthira's fame spread over the land.

At this stage friends began to advise him to perform the *Rajasuya* sacrifice, and to proclaim himself emperor of the country. This was a ceremonial sacrifice performed in those days by the monarch who felt himself to be the strongest and greatest in the country, whose rule extended over the widest area of land and over the greatest number of people.

But Yudhishthira knew that he must be sure of his strength before he could perform the *Rajasuya Yajna* and call himself emperor. If any ruler challenged his right to this name there would be trouble and war. Failure or defeat would easily make him an object of ridicule and scorn, and a prey to the schemes of jealous enemies.

"The Rajasuya Yajna is not to be lightly undertaken," said Yudhishthira. He spoke to Krishna about the matter and told him his doubts.

Krishna told him that there was one king in the country who would challenge his right to empire: that was Jarasandha, king of Magadha. Jarasandha was a tyrant and a threat to the whole world. Eighty-six princes captured by him in war lay in his prisons. Krishna told Yudhishthira that Jarasanda must be defeated before he could claim the title of the sovereign of the earth. But the peace-loving Yudhishthira drew back at the thought of enmity with another. He had no wish to pick quarrels with his neighbours, and he told Krishna so. "Let us give up the idea of the Rajasuya," he begged.

But Bhima and Arjuna thought differently. The quiet life of peace they led irked them, and they longed for action. They felt that it was their duty as Kshatriyas to make war upon the wicked and come to the help of the defenceless, and they told Yudhishthira so. They begged him to give them leave to lead their armies and march upon Jarasandha's city.

But Krishna knew that they would stand no chance against Jarasandha in an open war. "Your armies will be driven like chaff before the wind by those of Jarasandha!" he told them.

"What then?" Bhima and Arjuna asked, and Krishna told them that Jarasandha must be challenged to a duel. "He must be slain in a hand-to-hand fight," he said.

Yudhishthira listened to all this talk with misgivings in his heart. He was greatly distressed to see his brothers so eager for war and power, for he himself was a gentle soul, a man of peace, who would have been happy to leave his neighbours in peace, just as he would have been happy to be left alone. He did not care greatly for foolhardy adventure, for battles and quarrels. But Krishna argued long and persistently, and pointed out the danger in this world of allowing evil to grow. Then at last Yudhishthira was persuaded, and he agreed reluctantly to accompany Krishna and his brothers to Jarasandha's royal city in disguise.

CHAPTER XVI

THE SLAYING OF JARASANDHA

S THEY travelled to Girivraja, capital of Magadha, Krishna told the Pandava brothers the strange story of its ruler Jarasandha. Men said that he had been born not whole, as other people are born, but in two halves. But a medicine woman, whose name was Jara, had with the aid of magic, joined the two pieces together and restored the child to the grateful parents with her blessings.

She had blessed him with long life and superhuman strength. All men would fear him, she said. No weapons would touch him and he would excel in wrestling and in feats of strength.

But there would be one flaw in Jarasandha's strength: Jarasandha's body, which consisted of two separate fragments joined together, would fall apart easily. However, even this would not harm him. For as often as his body was torn in two, so often would the pieces come together and life would return to him. Neither would he

141

die until the pieces were so placed that they would never come together again.

Jarasandha grew up into a reckless and wilful man, ambitious for power, greedy for wealth, ruthless and cruel towards all who came in his way. He made war upon his neighbours, and his empire grew steadily in size and strength. So powerful indeed had Jarasandha become that Krishna himself had had to yield before the superior strength of his forces and retreat from his capital city Mathura to the very shores of the western sea, where he had to establish a new capital, Dwaraka. But in the east Jarasandha's empire swelled and his pride and wicked deeds grew with his power.

Krishna warned the Pandava brothers that Jarasandha was strong and cunning, and that it would not be easy to overpower him. He advised them to enter Girivraja in disguise, dressed as Brahmin priests.

The gates of Jarasandha's capital were heavily guarded. King Jarasandha had of late felt a strange anxiety: bad dreams had troubled his sleep and it had been foretold by sooth-sayers[1] that the days to come were inauspicious[2] for him

---

[1] People who have the power to look into the future.

[2] Not favourable; not lucky.

and filled with dangers of many kinds. For this reason he had ordered that the gates of the city as well as those of the royal palace should be guarded so that no enemy could enter to do him harm. He had invited Brahmin priests from far and near to come and perform sacrifices to please the gods. Knowing this, Krishna and the Pandavas had disguised themselves as Brahmin priests, and the guards, not recognizing them, had allowed them to pass. They entered the palace gates and stood among the Brahmins around the sacrificial fire. Nobody knew them and they were pleased that so far all had gone well with their plan. But as Jarasandha went among his guests to welcome them, he stopped before the Pandava brothers and looked at them curiously for a long time. He was suspicious. These men did not look like Brahmins and men of peace. He noticed that their hands were scarred and blistered, as if by the continual use of arms and weapons. He watched them carefully as they moved about, and very soon he guessed. He came to Bhima, and laughed out, "I have discovered you beneath your disguise, O Pandava! And you, Krishna, I have discovered you too. You are indeed at the root of all this!" Then, growing stern, he demanded to know what they wanted from him and why they had come.

"A duel, Jarasandha," cried Bhima, no longer able to keep up the pretence. "I wish to wrestle with you!"

Thus challenged, Jarasandha had no other honourable course open to him but to accept, and he did so, for he was no coward.

"Do you think I fear you, you brat?" he sneered, "Come, come! In a few minutes your bones will be ground to fine powder."

So saying, Jarasandha led them to the arena where wrestling matches were held, and there Bhima and he stood before each other in the ring, stripped to the waist. They were evenly matched. Yudhishthira, watching, prayed that all would go well; he wished in his heart that kingship had not carried with it so many burdens. News of the match spread quickly and the people flocked in great numbers to see it.

At the given signal they started advancing towards each other like bulls and came to grips. As they wrestled, it was difficult to tell who was the stronger of the two. Their strength and their skill seemed so evenly matched that if once Bhima overcame Jarasandha and threw him upon the floor, it was not long before Jarasandha

turned the tables upon Bhima, and dealt with
him in similar fashion. Each evening the heroes
would retire, neither victorious, neither vanquished, and the next morning the wrestling
would continue. Thus it went on for fourteen
days, and the people who watched saw victory
and defeat alternating with each other till it
seemed that the fight would never end. Then
one day, something happened; the wrestlers
had come to so close a grip that no one could
tell which limb was whose. It was a tense moment,
and in the silence could be heard only their
heavy breathing. Suddenly Bhima slipped his
hand out of Jarasandha's grip. In a trice he
caught his opponent's foot. He struggled from
Jarasandha's grasp, and quicker than it takes to
tell, threw him upon the floor. Then with a
mighty roar of triumph he put his foot upon the
fallen Jarasandha, and tearing him into two,
he flung the pieces away. "Victory! victory is
ours," he roared. But he cried out too soon!
For to his amazement, he saw the two pieces
move towards each other, until they joined together. And as soon as they touched each other,
Jarasandha was restored, and he rose up again,
ready to continue the fight. Three times did
Bhima tear Jarasandha into two pieces and three

times did the pieces join together making Jarasandha whole again, many times stronger even than he had been before. Bhima was non-plussed. He was growing tired. Never had he seen such a monster as this, who, even when torn apart and cleft in two, recovered his life and his strength.

They went into the fight again! Jarasandha laughed: "Surrender, O Bhima!" he roared. "Though I have eighty-six kings in my dungeons, there is still room for more, and nothing would please me better than to spare your life, and make you and your brothers my prisoners!"

"I have come here to wrestle, Jarasandha," Bhima roared back, "not to exchange words with you as women do. Come forward and fight .... Or have you had enough? Are you tired? If you are, shall I carry you now through the dust, to surrender before your visitors?"

For answer Jarasandha gave a whoop of anger, as he advanced again, arms stretched out, head bent like an angry bull's, muscles flexed.

Once more the fight began, and the two wrestled many rounds together, until once more Bhima caught his opponent by the legs and tore him into two. And at this moment, Krishna made a sign to Bhima. He took a betel leaf

146

between his thumb and finger, and tore it into two, and he crossed his hands before he threw the pieces away. Bhima took the hint and he too crossed his hands before he threw down the two halves of Jarasandha's body away, so that when the pieces moved they could only move farther from each other. They could not come together or join, and Jarasandha breathed his last breath and died at the hands of Bhima, and his evil rule came to an end.

Then the Pandavas went through the royal palace and down to the prison cells, where they set free Jarasandha's prisoners. The people of Magadha hailed the Pandavas who had freed them from their yoke, and blessed them with flowers and vermilion powder.

Jarasandha was cremated by the Pandava brothers. After the period of mourning was over, Yudhishthira placed Jarasandha's young son Sahadeva upon Magadha's throne, and he acknowledged Yudhishthira as his overlord.

This done, the Pandavas returned to Indraprastha.

CHAPTER XVII

YUDHISHTHIRA PERFORMS THE RAJASUYA SACRIFICE

WITH Jarasandha dead, the way was open to Yudhishthira to perform the Imperial Sacrifice, the Rajasuya Yajna, for there remained no one in the country now who could challenge his overlordship. Yudhishthira's hands were further strengthened by the alliance he had made with powerful rulers of the time. While he ruled in Indraprastha, Yudhishthira sent his brothers to travel around the country to meet chieftains and rulers of many tribes and they had all come forward, and had offered him their friendship, acknowledging Yudhishthira as their overlord.

Besides there was Drupada, king of the Panchalas, the father of their queen Draupadi and inveterate enemy of Drona. He was a staunch ally of the Pandavas.

Then there were Krishna and Balarama, the Yadava princes of Dwaraka. Their friendship with the Pandavas was deep and warm. And when Arjuna won for himself the love and the hand in marriage of their sister, Subadhra, this friendship was strengthened further by ties of relationship.

With powerful allies on all sides, and an empire of many subject states, Yudhishthira felt at last strong in his claim to the overlordship of the entire country. So upon the advice of those around him, he made preparations for the Rajasuya yajna. To this great ceremony were invited all the kings and princes of the realm, and they came to Indraprastha with presents and tribute, for to refuse the invitation would have been equal to an insult. All the rulers were there including Duryodhana of Hastinapura, Shakuni of Gandhara and Karna of Anga. Yudhishthira and his brothers welcomed their guests cordially, and showed each of them the honour and respect due to him. Every day there were festivities and ceremonies and celebrations, until the last day when Yudhishthira was to receive the imperial crown.

On that last day, however, an ugly quarrel arose which marred the beauty of the festivities of all those days, and cast a gloom over the city. On that day, Yudhishthira, wishing to do homage to each of the assembled princes in turn, according to their rank, led Krishna of Dwaraka to the foremost seat of honour.

Now Krishna was not, in that assembly, a king as the others were. It was his brother who was the crowned head of Dwaraka. For that matter, Dwaraka itself was not the foremost of the states represented there. Yudhishthira's action in giving Krishna the first place, therefore, surprised many people. It seemed to them to be a blunder, and there were several uplifted eye-brows as Krishna was led to the place of honour. But Yudhishthira had known what he was doing. He knew that Krishna was greater than all the people assembled there, though his greatness did not stem from material things like wealth; Krishna did not have the ordinary trappings of power. But Krishna was wise and godly. Yudhishthira felt that it was Krishna's wisdom and goodness that entitled him to the first place in the assembly.

But as Yudhishthira led Krishna to the first place there was a murmur of protest from among the guests. Complaints began to be voiced, softly at first and then louder, until Shishupala, King of Chedi, arose angrily from his seat. Shishupala hated Krishna bitterly; he could not bear to see him thus honoured. He broke out into such a volley of angry words against Krishna that the assembled people held their breath in fear. There were some however, who felt old jealousies rankle in their breasts again, and were secretly pleased.

Yudhishthira looked around him in dismay. After a while Bhishma arose and held up his hand for silence. He warned Shishupala sternly of the consequences of his behaviour, and related to the assembly a prophecy made at Shishupala's birth, that he would one day meet his death at Krishna's hands. Then he spoke to the assembled guests and told them how at his birth, Shishupala had come into the world with three eyes and four hands, and how soothsayers, looking into the future, had predicted an early and violent death for the boy. The slayer, they said, would be the person who would cure him of his deformity. Then the anxious parents had travelled around the country with the baby, but no one had been able to cure him until Krishna came one day and lifted up the child. At Krishna's touch the boy was cured. The extra limbs withered away and fell off. But the joy of the parents was clouded by the remembrance of the second half of the prophecy; they knew that

Krishna, who had healed their son, would also be his slayer. Then Shishupala's mother, who was also Krishna's aunt, fell at his feet and begged for mercy. "Though he may wrong you a hundred times, Lord, you must forgive him and spare his life." she sobbed. Krishna gave her his promise. "For your sake, gentle lady," he said, "I will forgive him a hundred wrongs. But he may over-reach himself, and the day may come when he may offend me once too often, and then he will force my hand!"

The queen knew then that in fairness she could not ask for more.

Shishupala grew up. Strange though it may seem, he hated Krishna, who had healed him, as fiercely as only evil can hate the good. Hearing Bhishma relate this story, Shishupala grew even angrier than before. He advanced before the assembly and continued to shout against Krishna, insulting him and calling him names. The assembled people sat tensely in their places; a few tried to stop Shishupala, but in vain. Meanwhile, Krishna sat in his seat, unruffled and silent, looking at the angry youth with calm eyes. Krishna's lips were moving. Shishupala did not know it, but Krishna was counting each insult that he was flinging at him. When he had counted a hundred, he stood up and held up his hand, and commanded him to stop, warning him of the consequences of going too far. But Shishupala's hatred made him reckless, and for answer he only gave Krishna a dark look and flung at him another vile term of abuse. But he did not get very far. For at this insult which was the hundred and first, Krishna threw at him his shining discus. Before the eyes of the assembled people it flew across the great hall, flashing like a streak of lightning, and the next moment, Shishupala lay upon the floor, his neck slashed from his body, and his blood flowing in a dark stream over the floor of the hall.

A stunned silence fell upon the assembly. The friends of Shishupala looked fearfully at Krishna, but no one raised a voice, for they knew that he had brought this upon himself.

Shishupala's funeral rites were performed at Yudhishthira's command. Yudhishthira ordered that he be given the funeral honours due to a warrior and a king. All the great personages there followed Shishupala's bier upon the last journey, and they mourned for him. He had been a hot-headed and misguided youth, but it could not be denied that he had been a brave prince.

The funeral over, Yudhishthira took up again the performance of the sacrifice which had so rudely been interrupted, and the festivities continued to the chanting of hymns and prayers. Holy water was sprinkled upon Yudhishthira's head; his body was anointed with perfumed oil, and he was crowned Emperor. The elders who were assembled there came and blessed him, and the younger people did him homage as he sat upon the imperial throne.

But Yudhishthira's heart was heavy and he was full of foreboding. The future seemed to him to be dark and uncertain. The killing of Shishupala had been like a stain on that beautiful day. Around him he saw the dark unsmiling faces of his cousins, the Kauravas. There was so much hatred and hostility around him that he began to doubt if, after all, kingship and empire were worthwhile things. He resolved then and there that he, as king or emperor, would never start a quarrel with any one of his own accord, and would do nothing to provoke a war Always he would seek to keep peace, whatever the cost. But still his heart continued to be heavy and uneasy.

CHAPTER XVIII

SHAKUNI MAKES HIS APPEARANCE

HE Rajasuya sacrifice completed, the guests went home to their different cities. But Duryodhana stayed on in Indraprastha for a while at his cousin's invitation. Yudhishthira showered him with kindness and courtesy and entertained him royally in the palace. He was taken around the capital and shown its wonderful sights. But when Duryodhana saw all the things that the Pandavas had built, when he saw how from the four corners of the empire came vast quantities of tribute to the overlord,—gold and silver and pearls and precious stones; perfumes and incense; grains and cereals; metal ware and crystals and articles of wood and ivory; silk and muslin cloth and the furs of rare animals, woollen shawls and carpets and leather goods; camels and horses, elephants and peacocks— when Duryodhana saw how hundreds of people waited upon Yudhishthira's word, and how

thousands of slaves bent low before him, and how his subjects praised him and honoured him and loved him, his jealousy smouldered afresh like a fire that was fanned to new life. He went about the palace sulky and out of temper, nursing his anger and feeling very sorry for himself, and as he wandered in and out of the corridors, he found that the palace was so vast and so cunningly built, that he could not easily find his way around. Its magnificence quite took his breath away, for in all his life he had not seen anything like it. As he wandered, it seemed to him that he saw a pool of water before him, whereupon he carefully picked up his clothes to avoid getting them wet, only to find that there was no water there at all. The floor had been polished so smoothly that it had only *seemed* like water. He felt rather foolish and hoped no one had seen him, but at that moment Nakula passed by and explained to him how there was no water at all there. His tone was kind enough, but Duryodhana was sure he saw the glint of amusement in Nakula's eyes. Further on, Duryodhana blundered again, mistaking a crystal door for open space and bumping his head into it, so that tears sprang to his eyes— whereupon Bhima emerged from out of no-

At that moment Nakula passed by and explained
to him how there was no water at all there.

where (or so it seemed) and held the door open
for him, looking greatly concerned; but Duryodhana knew of course that Bhima was really
laughing.

A little while later Duryodhana landed with
a splash in a lotus pool which he had not seen,
and as he came up coughing and spluttering
and clutching his wet clothes, he heard the
giggling of women and saw behind a latticed
door, Draupadi and her ladies-in-waiting. They
fled when he saw them, but he heard their
laughter as he made his way to his apartment.

Duryodhana gnashed his teeth with rage. The
thought of the prosperity of the Pandavas was
like a thorn in his flesh. Secure on his throne,
Yudhishthira had built up a powerful empire
and strengthened himself with many alliances.

His power was so great that Duryodhana knew
that there was no armed might that could hurt
him or bring him down. Yudhishthira had escaped every trap that Duryodhana had laid
for him and now he was emperor. Duryodhana
could not sleep for his jealousy. Bitter thoughts
filled his mind and he had no joy in living.

If only, he thought, if only the Pandavas
could be destroyed! How he would love to see
Yudhishthira's empire come crumbling down;

how he would love to see Yudhishthira and his
brothers reduced to beggary! But Duryodhana
knew that in the normal course of things this
would never happen.

He returned to Hastinapura to his loving
parents, to his kingdom and people. But his
mood did not improve. Indeed the sight of his
own surroundings, so poor and ordinary in
comparison to his cousin's, only increased the
depth of his misery. Discontent, hatred, and
envy made him a very unhappy man indeed.

But as he brooded in this manner there came
to him one who had the sly, slinking ways of a
jackal: Shakuni was Duryodhana's maternal
uncle, the brother of Gandhari and the prince
of Gandhara. Shakuni did not love Duryodhana,
for Duryodhana had done him much harm.
Once long ago, he had seized Shakuni and his
ninety-nine brothers and put them into a prison
cell. There they had languished while Duryodhana gloated over their fate. He sent them
food that was just enough for one person to
live on. When the gaoler brought it, they fell
upon it like a pack of wolves to devour it—one
man's portion for a hundred men. But there was
one among them who saw how this would destroy
all of them.

"Let such a thing not happen," he said. "Let one man among us be fed and let him live, and one day when the ninety-nine of us are gone, this one will avenge our cruel death." So they cast lots and Shakuni's name was drawn. Then the brothers called out to Shakuni and declared that he must be the one to live and avenge their death. Shakuni wept. One by one he embraced his brothers and solemnly vowed that he would destroy Duryodhana. Then he ate the food that was sent, while his brothers died slowly of hunger. One after another they died, while he held them in his arms, and with their dying eyes they begged him to remember his promise. Shakuni never forgot. When Duryodhana found that ninety-nine of the princes were dead, he had Shakuni released. Thereafter Shakuni lived at his nephew's palace.

He moved about the palace corridors like an evil shadow, smirking and whispering, and he kept Duryodhana company. While they were together, he fawned upon him and flattered him and continued to poison Duryodhana's heart and fan the flames of his jealousy and anger.

"You must not despair!" he whispered to his nephew. "Yudhishthira and his brothers can be destroyed." "How?" cried Duryodhana morosely.

"They have vast armies and loyal subjects. Their power is much greater than ours."

"Never you fear!" Shakuni answered him, grinning an evil grin. "There are other ways of destroying a man, where armed might is of no avail. It is true that Yudhishthira will never be defeated on the battle-field, but his downfall can be brought about by cunning and guile."

Duryodhana pricked up his ears, and Shakuni drew nearer and whispered:

"Invite Yudhishthira here to a game of dice," he said. "You know that Yudhishthira has a weakness for gambling with dice. I will play for you against him. I will play skilfully and if necessary, I will cheat too at the game. I will stop at nothing to win from Yudhishthira the stakes that he will offer; I will goad him into staking all his possessions, even to his kingdom and his subjects. By doing so, I will bring him to his ruin."

Duryodhana was delighted. It seemed to him an excellent way by which to defeat Yudhishthira and lay him low. Then a doubt arose in his mind. He had heard that Yudhishthira, knowing the evils gambling brought, had, when he became king, taken an oath never to touch

the dice or gamble. Duryodhana reminded
Shakuni of this. But Shakuni chuckled, rubbing
his hands together. "What is the oath of a
gambler?" he said contemptuously, and his
nephew nodded, smiling in agreement.

And so the two put their heads together and
hatched the plot. Yudhishthira was to be
persuaded to come to a gambling match. Shakuni
was to play against him and, by fair means or
foul, as it suited him, to defeat him at each
round and win from him all his possessions until
he was reduced to nothing; and then he and
his brothers were to be driven into exile!

CHAPTER XIX

VIDURA GOES TO INDRAPRASTHA

URYODHANA thought over Shakuni's words and laid his plans with care. When he felt the time was ripe, he came to his blind old father, Dhritarashtra, to get his consent to the whole scheme. But as Dhritarashtra listened to what his son had to say, he grew uneasy and afraid. His conscience told him that what his son planned to do was neither right nor wise. But at the same time the old man was not unwilling in his heart to see the success of his son's plan. He tried at first, though rather half-heartedly, to persuade Duryodhana to change his mind.

But of course Duryodhana would not heed the old man. He treated his advice with contempt and brushed it aside. He argued at length with his father to make him believe that what he planned to do was not wrong. He fretted and fumed and sulked and stormed until at last the weak Dhritarashtra gave him permission to invite Yudhishthira to the gambling match.

Duryodhana was beside himself with joy. He had a great hall of pleasure built especially for the gambling match. He ordered a palace to be made for the Pandavas to stay in when they came. He thought out his whole wicked plan very carefully in his mind. Deciding that the best person to take his invitation to the Pandavas was Vidura, Duryodhana had him summoned before Dhritarashtra. The old king commanded Vidura to go down to Indraprastha to the Pandavas with the invitation to the gambling match. When Vidura heard this he was shocked, for he saw through Duryodhana's plan. He spoke out his mind quite frankly and sternly and advised the king to stop this folly before it was too late.

"What you seem to be planning is not only wicked but foolish and dangerous as well," he warned.

But Dhritarashtra was weak and stupid. He was like clay in the hands of his son. Besides he did not like Vidura, who was only a commoner of humble birth, to tell him, the king, what to do. So he drew himself up rather haughtily upon his throne and commanded Vidura to go. "Your sovereign commands you," said Dhritarashtra coldly, and Vidura bowed his head, for he knew he must obey the word of the king.

As he moved away, Dhritarashtra murmured to him, "This is fate; all is fate. No man can change fate. What has to happen will happen."

But Vidura sighed heavily and made no answer. He knew that men blame fate because they lack courage to act rightly. When their foolish actions result in disaster, then they sit back and blame fate when they should in fairness blame only themselves. Vidura looked at Dhritarashtra with reproach in his eye but he said nothing.

Soon afterwards he set off for Indraprashtha. A warm welcome awaited him at the palace of the Pandavas. But Vidura remained sad and spoke little. At last Yudhishthira asked him what the matter was, and Vidura told him of the invitation he had brought for the gambling match.

Yudhishthira listened gravely.

"Men bring ruin upon themselves by such play," he answered slowly. "Has it not been said that wise men do not play games of chance? Why does Duryodhana seek this kind of war with us? Is it not more honourable for a Kshatriya prince to stand upon the battle-field and fight than to gamble at a dice board?"

But even as he spoke these words of wisdom Yudhishthira was already wavering, and in his heart the desire to gamble which he had held in check for so many days, began to stir and awaken again.

His resolution weakened; for Yudhishthira loved the dice. He began to find excuses for breaking the vow he had made years ago never to touch the gambling board.

"A Kshatriya may not refuse a challenge," he murmured. "It would look like cowardice. And then what harm could there be in an innocent game?" Then again—"It would be awkward to refuse an invitation to play. They would laugh at me as a coward. Worse, they might be offended, and that might lead to the very quarrel I wish to avoid."

"I will come," he said at last. "It will be neither right nor courteous to refuse." His brothers tried to hold him back, but Yudhishthira would not heed their advice. The lure of the gambling board was too much for him. He found a hundred reasons why he must go to Hastinapura to play, and he allowed himself to fall into the trap that Duryodhana and Shakuni had laid for him.

CHAPTER XX

THE GAMBLING MATCH

T IS said that the dice that were used in that fateful gambling match that Yudishthira played in Hastinapura, had been made out of the bones of the ninety-nine brothers of Shakuni who had died in prison. When they had died and their flesh had been reduced to ash, Shakuni had taken their bones and whittled them and carved them and made them the most beautiful and seductive[1] dice that were ever seen. And into these had gone the fierce hot desire for revenge of the dead men. Shakuni hid away the dice where no man could see them, and kept them until the day of the gambling match.

As they journeyed on their way to Hastinapura, the Pandava brothers were heavy-hearted and anxious, for they knew only too well of Yudhishthira's love of gambling. They knew too

---

[1] To seduce is to lead astray, entice or charm away. So *seductive* is anything which entices, leads away or charms.

that Duryodhana's invitation could not have been prompted by any friendly feelings. But they said nothing, for Yudhishthira was their king as well as their elder brother and they could only advise him. They could not forbid him to do what he chose to do.

Yudhishthira was not without his own doubts. He had given in to Duryodhana partly because it would have seemed impolite to refuse and partly also because he loved the game. He was sure in his mind, in the manner of gamblers, that he would win, but he was not sure at all whether he had done right in accepting to play.

Duryodhana was all smiles as he welcomed his cousins. He took care to see that they were fed and feasted and made comfortable.

On the day fixed for the gambling match the Pandava brothers came to the newly-built hall where all was in readiness for the game to start. Duryodhana stood waiting impatiently near by. Shakuni stood clutching the dice in his hands. His small eyes gleamed like a rat's. Around the hall sat the men of the great Kuru clan, the royal family and their ministers, the councillors, the teachers and all the high officials. Their faces were full of anxiety as they waited for the drama to begin. They had all tried to draw Duryodhana away from the evil path he was taking. They had talked to him about the duty and the code of a Kshatriya, reminding him that a true warrior fights upon the battle-field and does not seek victory in games of chance. And Bhishma had warned him that he was letting loose forces of evil which would one day overtake him and bring about his ruin. "Do you not understand that the result of evil action can only be evil?" he pleaded, speaking both to Duryodhana and Dhritarashtra. But Duryodhana tossed his proud head scornfully. He would have none of the old man's advice. "Yudhishthira has accepted my invitation," he said angrily. "What is there in a friendly match?"

Drona and Bhishma sat now with the blind king and watched in silence as the Pandavas came in. Yudhishthira's eye was troubled as he greeted the assembled people. "Gambling is evil," he murmured. But when Duryodhana taunted him with wanting to go back on his word, Yudhishthira took his seat at the gambling board and called out to Duryodhana to come and begin the game. He did not wish people to think he was scuttling. But Duryodhana answered, "Shakuni, my uncle will play for me. I shall sit beside him and his losses will be my losses as his gains will be my gains."

Yudhishthira looked up quickly: "This is not fair," he protested. "This was not part of the agreement. I did not come to play against Shakuni." For Yudhishthira knew how sharp Shakuni was, how cunning and clever and also how unscrupulous. Shakuni cared nothing for principles, for right and for wrong. He cared only for his own self-interest. To get his advantage Shakuni would stoop to any evil. Yudhishthira knew this, and when he heard that this shrewd and cunning man was to play against him, he protested.

But Duryodhana laughed and taunted him again, asking him if he was afraid of losing. Duryodhana's words were like a challenge to Yudhishthira, as indeed he had meant them to be.

"I am not afraid," Yudhishthira said proudly, "Though you do not play fair, I shall play with you." Duryodhana was pleased. They sat down to play.

Yudhishthira laid his stake upon the board. It was a necklace of rich and rare pearls which he wore; he took the dice and flung them down.

Then Shakuni rattled his dice and played. At the end of the first round Shakuni had won, and Yudhishthira handed over to him the stake. He had lost his pearl necklace. But what of that? His treasure-chests were full of money and rare jewels. The game was only beginning. At the next round Yudhishthira staked the jewellery in his treasury. They played, and he lost again.

"The jewels in your treasury are mine now," said Shakuni softly. Yudhishthira laughed. The excitement was mounting to his head. Nothing daunted, he played again. He staked the gold and silver in his treasure houses, and these also he lost. They continued to play: one by one Yudhishthira staked his chariots and his elephants and horses; he pledged his cattle; then his slaves and his servants. One by one at every round he lost some treasure or other. A strange and evil fate seemed to dog him upon that luckless day. Shakuni's crafty eyes gleamed. The dice seemed to obey him: he was well pleased. Shakuni was an adept at the game. Besides he cheated without shame.

"Will you continue to play?" Duryodhana taunted his cousin as he watched him lose again and again and again. Yudhishthira answered, breathing hard, stung by the mockery in his voice; "Yes, I will continue." For now he was seized with a kind of madness and he would not stop. He must win: somehow he would win. He would not give up until he had made good all his losses.

He played again. This time, he pledged the wealth of his kingdom, his horses and elephants and camels, the villages of his empire and all his people, and one by one he lost all the things he staked.

Day after day the game went on, Yudhishthira pledging, one after another, his worldly possessions and losing them to Shakuni. And still he would not stop. Then the dark hour came when he had staked and lost all and had nothing left of his own; he was like a penniless beggar in the street. But even then he would not give up.

His brothers crept up to him slowly and begged, "It is enough, O brother! Come, let us go; there is nothing left for us now to stake."

Yudhishthira hardly heard them. He stretched out his trembling hand for the dice.

"I will still win back all I have lost!" he cried, looking around him wildly. His eye lighted upon his brothers and suddenly he cried out, "I pledge now my brother, the handsome Sahadeva."

In the hall the people held their breath. A royal prince was being used as a pawn in the game! A human being had been staked as if he were a chattel! But nothing mattered to Yudhishthira. It seemed as if he had taken leave of his senses. He rattled the dice in the cup and threw it down—and he lost. Once more he lost!

"Ha," chuckled Shukani softly. "Sahadeva is lost. Now he is our slave!"

Yudhishthira clenched his teeth; no one moved in their seats as Sahadeva was led to where Shakuni sat. "What will you pledge now? Sahadeva is gone! Will you not try to recover him?" Shakuni whispered, leering.

Yudhishthira answered speaking hoarsely: "I have lost Sahadeva. But Nakula is there. Nakula, who is skilled in the arts; Nakula, who is the best horseman in the country. I pledge Nakula. With him as my stake I shall win back what I have lost." Nakula came forward and he too was lost in that desperate game. Shakuni laughed. "The game must stop now!" he taunted Yudhishthira. "Surely you will not pledge your full brothers. You can afford to give away the sons of Madri who are only your half brothers, but naturally the sons of Kunti would be too precious?"

Yudhishthira answered hotly: "My brothers are all equally dear to me!" he cried. "Prove it then!" Shakuni challenged, and Yudhishthira fell into the trap. "I will pledge Bhima!" he said, I will prove to you that the sons of Kunti are not dearer to me than the sons of Madri!"

Again they played, and again with the same result, for Bhima too was lost.

Shakuni's eyes glittered with his greed. He leaned forward. "And now, Yudhishthira? Who now?"

"Arjuna!" Yudhishthira cried, despair in his eyes and big cold drops of sweat upon his forehead. His voice sounded strange and shrill. His hands trembled violently as he held them out for the dice.

"I will win yet. All that I have lost I will win," he thought desperately.

But he lost Arjuna too.

All his faithful brothers had been pledged and lost, and Yudhishthira was alone.

"Yudhishthira! What now?" Shakuni mocked, relentlessly, leering at him.

"Myself!" Yudhishthira cried out, "I will

pledge myself and win. I will win all that I have lost." But when Yudhishthira played, he lost again, and now he and all his four brothers were the slaves of Shakuni.

Still Shakuni would not let him stop. He leaned forward and reminded him that there was Draupadi still who had not been staked.

"It may be that she will bring you good luck today!" he whispered.

Then the desperate Yudhishthira cried out, his voice choking with sobs, and his tears flowing, "Draupadi! I pledge Draupadi this time!"

All this while there had been a tense silence in the assembly while the people sat, looking helplessly on, while Yudhishthira gambled away his own liberty and that of his brothers. But now the silence was broken with loud shouts of protest.

"Do not do this!" they cried out. "For shame, Yudhishthira! Stop the game, Duryodhana! Stop Shakuni! A woman may not be thus dishonoured."

But Yudhishthira clutched at the dice in his hand as a drowning man would clutch at a straw. He would not stop now. The blood pounding in his head, his heart racing within him, Yudhishthira played, this time with Draupadi as a stake. And once again he lost.

Then Duryodhana rose up, laughing aloud in his pride, and commanded Vidura to go and fetch Draupadi. "From now on she is our slave!" he said. "She shall sweep the palace floors!"

But Vidura refused to go. He spoke out his mind sternly and openly to Duryodhana, and warned him of the disaster that would surely overtake him if he continued in his evil ways. Other people spoke too, among whom was Vikarna, the youngest of Duryodhana's brothers, reproaching him for the wrong he was doing.

But Duryodhana's triumph had gone to his head, and he would heed no one. Since Vidura would not go, Duryodhana sent his charioteer to fetch Draupadi from her apartments. But when the charioteer came before Draupadi, the proud princess refused to go with him.

"Go and tell them," she said, holding her head high, "that Yudhishthira was a slave already when he pledged me as a stake in his game. As a slave he has no rights and no belongings. The instant Yudhishthira became a slave I ceased to be his wife. Therefore, since I did not belong to him, he had no right to use me as his pawn!" Gathering up her silken skirts, pride and anger flashing in her dark eyes, Draupadi ordered Duryodhana's charioteer out of the house.

"Go and tell your master I will not come." she said.

When Duryodhana heard what the charioteer had to say, and when he saw how he was thwarted, he commanded his brother Dushahsana to go and bring Draupadi before them. Dushahsana did not hesitate. At his brother's bidding he arose and swaggered out of the hall, boasting that he would drag the proud Draupadi through the dust and bring her to her knees before them.

He went to the apartments of Draupadi, calling out to her in a mocking voice, and he followed her into the inner rooms where she fled from him. He caught her by her long dark hair, and dragged her out of the house, down the steps and through the dust into his chariot. And he brought her thus into the hall before Duryodhana and forced her to her knees before him.

But she, proud woman, rose up again and stood before the assembly, her hair streaming behind her, and her large eyes flaming. She spoke to the elders before her and declared to them that she was no slave, for Yudhishthira had already lost his freedom when he had pledged her. And in a clear, ringing voice, she reproached them for the wrongs they had allowed to be done.

But the world seemed to have fallen on evil days, for they only bent their heads, hearing her, and her protests went unheeded in that goodly company.

Duryodhana's pride and wickedness had gone beyond all bounds. He had neither pity now nor mercy nor good sense. In his madness he ordered that the very clothes that Draupadi wore should be stripped from her as she stood in the assembly; for he thought that this would be the best way to disgrace the proud Draupadi and bring her to shame.

When he gave the order, a great shout went up in the assembly, and the elders begged Duryodhana to desist from such madness. Even Dhritarashtra added his weak voice to their protests. But Duryodhana's heart seemed to be made of stone. Nothing would move him. With an arrogant laugh he commanded Dushahsana to tear Draupadi's clothing away.

In a daze, Draupadi heard the order as she stood in that assembly, alone and helpless. Fear filled her. Suddenly she knew that there was no one who could come to her aid in the whole world save God—neither the five stalwart princes who were her husbands and who loved her, nor the wealthy glittering nobles and courtiers, nor the wise elders of Dhritarashtra's court, nor even the King himself. No one would or could come to her help. In that terrible moment of distress Draupadi turned all her thoughts to God, and she cried out to Him for help, knowing Him to be man's final refuge.

It is related how the Lord Krishna then came to her rescue and worked a miracle upon that day, for as Dushahsana stripped her of one garment, another one appeared upon her, and as that was torn away another came in its place, and another and another and another—and so on endlessly. Dushahsana's swarthy hands grew tired as he pulled. Rivers of sweat ran down his face and body; and the pile of garments he had pulled from Draupadi grew so high that it reached the ceiling. All who sat there looking on were stunned. But Draupadi knew nothing at all of what took place. For she stood rooted to the spot, her eyes closed, her hands clasped, while all her thoughts and all her being were with God.

As Dushashana stripped her of one garment, another
appeared upon her.

The Gambling Match

It is said that in the end Dushahsana grew so faint and tired that he had to stop. Then Draupadi opened her eyes, and as she did so the great pile of glittering garments went up in flames, and nothing was left of them except smoke and ashes.

All this while the Pandava brothers stood helpless. Their wife had been dishonoured and they had been powerless to protect her. They hung their heads in shame and sorrow. The mighty Bhima felt his heart breaking. His great frame shook: he gnashed his teeth and clenched his hands and lifting up his voice he swore a great oath, declaring that the day would come when he would tear open the wicked Dushahsana's breast with his bare hands, and drink his blood.

As these happenings took place within, there came from outside the fearful sound of asses braying and vultures screeching; a wild wind rose up; the sky grew dark with an eclipse and a great storm burst. Hearing these sounds and recognizing them to be omens of evil, the blind Dhritarashtra grew pale and began to tremble. For now he was thoroughly frightened by the extent of his son's folly.

Dhritarashtra was feeble. He could not say

"No" to his wayward son; but he could not ignore the stern warnings of the counsellors or the voice of his own conscience. When Duryodhana was absent for a while, Dhritarashtra summoned Draupadi before him and began to cajole her with soft and kind words, trying to soothe her great anger. He asked her to name whatever she wished, and promised that he would give it to her. At that, Draupadi stood before him with her head held high and her eyes proud and fearless, and demanded from him the freedom of Yudhishthira, her husband.

Dhritarashtra was only too glad to grant her her wish.

"Ask more, child," he begged her. "Ask more and you shall have your desire."

Then Draupadi spoke again and asked for the Pandava brothers to be set free, and that their arms and weapons be restored to them. Dhritarashtra, anxious to undo the wrongs his son had done, hastened to give the order to set the Pandavas free.

"Ask more, child, ask more!" he continued to wheedle. "Ask for your husband's kingdom."

But this Draupadi would not do. "A Kshatriya may ask for two gifts only and no more," she answered haughtily, "and I will ask no more. I do not want a kingdom as a gift from my enemies. My husbands are free men now. Armed with their weapons they can conquer the world."

Her words and the voice in which they were uttered made the old king quail.

"Nevertheless, even though you do not ask for it, the kingdom of Indraprastha is yours," he quavered in a persuasive tone. He begged the Pandavas to accept the offer and return to their kingdom in peace. He begged their forgiveness for the wrongs Duryodhana had done them, pleading with them to forget what had happended.

Draupadi did not answer at all. Only her eyes blazed fire as she left the hall. Her five husbands went with her.

So the Pandavas left the assembly hall, free men again because of Draupadi's courage, for it was she who had won them their freedom. For once Dhritarashtra had acted with some courage and firmness. He had taken his decision when Duryodhana had been absent for a while.

When Duryodhana returned, however, and heard what had happened, he was furious.

"What a foolish thing is this that you have done!" he stormed at his father. "What madness is this? You have set free enemies whom we have

insulted and dishonoured. Can you not see that
they will have their revenge?"

"What shall I do, then?" Dhritarashtra began
to whimper, frightened again by his son's words.
He was like a leaf in his weakness, blown about
by every wind. Then Duryodhana asked his
father to send for the Pandavas again for a
second game of dice. At that the people in the
assembly all cried out, "No, no, not again!"
Now at least let there be peace!"

But Duryodhana was headstrong and foolish
and must have his way.

"We shall play one more round," he announced. "This time the loser shall go into the
forest for twelve years and live there as an
ascetic. The thirteenth year, he shall spend in
disguise and hiding. If he should, during that
thirteenth year, be discovered or recognized,
then he shall spend twelve more years in the
forests."

It was a strange wager. Nobody had heard
of such a thing before. Everyone in the assembly,
even the valiant Karna, begged Duryodhana to
give up his madness and allow the Pandavas to
go in peace. But the advice fell on deaf ears,
and Duryodhana prevailed upon his father to
agree to this fantastic proposal.

So messengers were sent once more to the Pandavas. The five princes and their wife were still upon the road and had not reached Indraprastha yet. The messengers soon overtook them.

You would have thought that after the misfortunes he had brought upon himself and his family, Yudhishthira would have learnt wisdom and prudence. But strange to say, he had not. The love of the dice was as strong in him as ever. He did not like the thought that he owed his freedom and that of his brothers to Dhritarashtra's favour. He wanted to play and win. He felt luck would still favour him if he tried once more. His brothers cried out in despair, begging him not to accept, but Yudhishthira said:

"I will come and play one more round."

There was no dissuading him. He seemed to be bent on his own destruction. Sadly the Pandava brothers turned back and came once more to Hastinapura.

Once more, while his brothers looked on in gloomy silence, Yudhishthira played; and once more as he had done before, he lost. And now, in accordance with the terms of their wager, the Pandavas had to go into exile.

Then the Pandava princes and Draupadi rose

up with grim, set faces and bowed before the elders. They walked slowly out of the hall, heads bent, eyes lowered, speaking not a word, and all stood silent watching them go. But when they reached the street there came before them great crowds of weeping, sorrowful people who cried out and begged them not to go. Their weeping and their lamentations were so loud that in the hall, where he sat upon his throne, the blind Dhritarashtra heard them and trembled with fear.

Even the strong-willed Duryodhana began to feel uneasy and fearful of the future. He came running to Drona and begged him with tears in his eyes never to forsake him.

"I will stand by you, O Prince," Drona said wearily, "for I have eaten of your rice and I owe you loyalty. But what you have done is wrong." Drona spoke frankly and pointed out to Duryodhana the foolishness of his action. He counselled him to undo it by making peace with the Pandavas and returning to them their kingdom. Duryodhana turned away from him angrily.

"Make peace with my cousins!" he cried. "This I will never do."

He strode out of the hall turning upon his heel and the council came to an abrupt end.

CHAPTER XXI

THE PANDAVAS IN EXILE

HEN the news of the Pandavas' banishment reached Drupada, he hurried to meet them, accompanied by his son Dhrishtadyumna. Krishna too came quickly to their side, full of concern at the things that had taken place. At the sight of them the memory of her sufferings and the wrongs done to her returned to Draupadi in waves of grief. Weeping bitterly, she related to them the story of Duryodhana's evil deeds, of the gambling match and of how she had been dragged into the assembly and shamed. Hearing her, Dhrishtadyumna's face grew dark with anger. He took her trembling hands in his own and drawing her to him, he swore to her before all who were present, that he would avenge the wrongs she had suffered, even though he might die for it. Krishna spoke too, promising her that those who had caused her sorrow and brought about her disgrace would surely be destroyed.

Then Drupada and Dhrishtadyumna returned to Panchala, taking with them the young sons of Draupadi, and Krishna returned to Dwaraka with his sister Subadhra, wife of Arjuna, and her infant son Abhimanyu. Abhimanyu grew up in his uncle's home in Dwaraka.

The exiled Pandavas made their way into the forests where they were to spend the days of their banishment. Travelling westwards, they reached the wild, unexplored territory called the Kamyaka region on the banks of the river Saraswati. No Aryan except for a few rishis and hermits had ever set foot here before. Scattered here and there in the clearings of the forests and upon the banks of the rivers, they came across their hermitages and ashramas, and from time to time they stopped in these peaceful surroundings to visit the good and wise men.

Life was hard in the wilderness. But the Pandavas were brave and stout-hearted. Draupadi went with them wherever they went, sharing their hardships. In her heart the memory of the sorrows and humiliations she had suffered remained fresh and raw. She would never forget the wrongs the Kauravas had done her, neither would she let her husbands forget. She did not think much of Yudhishthira's meek and submissive behaviour, and she was often impatient with Arjuna too for the manner in which he allowed his elder brother to impose his authority. Bhima was more after her heart. For Bhima thought and felt like her.

From the Kamyaka forest they travelled to the Diavatvana lake on the banks of which they lived for five years. Then from here they went on to the holy site of Prayag, then eastwards again until they came to the eastern ocean, and after they had lived in these regions, they travelled back again and lived for a while in the forests of the Vindhyas. As they walked through the wilderness they discussed among themselves ways and means by which they would get back the kingdom Duryodhana had wrested from them.

Duryodhana had driven them into exile, and he now ruled over their domains. Duryodhana was greedy and cunning. The Pandavas did not think that he would return their kingdom to them at the end of their period of exile without a struggle. There would be a dispute which would surely lead to war. They knew they must arm themselves now and strengthen themselves with the alliances of friendly rulers.

In the meanwhile they lived the life of hermits

and as they wandered from place to place they came to know the surrounding country and its people well.

*   *   *   *   *

Far away in Hastinapura, Duryodhana's heart still burned with jealousy and allowed him no peace. One day he called to him Shakuni and Karna, and told them of a plan he had to destroy the Pandavas.

"Unarmed and helpless they wander through the forests," he said, "and if we attack them now, we shall certainly defeat them." Shakuni and Karna were delighted with the plan. The three of them agreed to keep the elders in the dark as to their real intention.

"Let us pretend that we are going to our cattle stations to count our cattle," Duryodhana suggested and the others applauded him warmly.

Then, having secured the necessary permission from his father and the elders at court, Duryodhana and his companions set out in high spirits from Hastinapura and arrived at the Daivatvana forest where the Pandavas lived in exile. But when they tried to enter it they found their way barred, for there, guarding the forest and the

Pandavas within, stood the heavenly armies of the Gandharvas under their King Chitrasena. Indra, who had seen Duryodhana's evil intention, had commanded them to protect the Pandavas. Duryodhana and his companions had thus to do battle with these heavenly warriors first. He had not foreseen this. His army, taken as it was by surprise, was completely routed by Chitrasena. Karna and Shakuni fled. Duryodhana was taken prisoner and dragged in disgrace before Yudhishthira.

When Yudhishthira saw his cousin in chains and thoroughly humbled, he pitied him. He begged Chitrasena to release him and, turning to his brothers who were clamouring for revenge, he reminded them that Duryodhana was after all their cousin and flesh of their flesh. "We cannot forsake him in his distress," said the gentle Yudhishthira. He ordered Duryodhana to be released, and speaking to him kindly, gave him permission to return to Hastinapura.

Duryodhana gnashed his teeth as he turned to go. There was no joy in his heart and no gratitude. His anger against the Pandavas increased a hundred-fold, for he hated to have to be thankful to them whom he considered his greatest enemies on earth.

Back in the palace he sulked and brooded all day, refusing to eat or drink or sleep. Karna tried to console him and rouse his broken spirit, but Duryodhana turned heavily away.

"Better far to die," he groaned, "than to owe my life to the man I hate."

Then Karna, grieved to see his friend so unhappy, swore to him a great and terrible oath, declaring that the day would come when he would surely destroy Arjuna. By his honour he swore, and by all that he held dear, that he would live the life of an ascetic, eating no meat and drinking no wine until he had killed Arjuna.

"If Arjuna is removed," said Karna, "the strength of the Pandavas will be cut at the root!"

Duryodhana's fainting heart lifted at Karna's words. He embraced his loyal friend warmly.

"We will defeat the Pandavas yet," he cried. "We will vanquish them and lay them low."

*   *   *   *   *

But the Pandavas, serving their term of exile in the forest, were learning much and growing rich in experience and wisdom. As they wandered they had many strange adventures.

Once a Rishi spoke to them and advised them

to obtain from the gods certain heavenly weapons which would be useful to them in the time to come. Arjuna, who was always ready for adventure, took him at his word. He took leave of his wife and brothers and set off alone for the Himalayan regions, where he hoped to do penance to please the gods and so obtain their weapons from them.

Armed with his bow, his quiver of arrows slung on his back, Arjuna walked through the forests alone for many long and weary days, suffering many hardships. He learned from his heavenly father, Indra, who revealed himself to him, that he would be given the weapons of the gods only if he could obtain the blessing of Mahadeva, the three-eyed God of Destruction. Then Arjuna made a clay image of Mahadeva and sat upon a rock before it in deep meditation. For many days he prayed and did hard penance. He grew so thin that the bones showed in his body, and his beard grew matted and long, and the clothing fell from him in tatters until he was naked in the Himalayan winter. At last Mahadeva appeared before him in the guise of a forest tribesman. But before he revealed himself, Mahaveda, wishing to test him, challenged Arjuna to a fight and the latter accepted the challenge; for all his prayer and meditation, for all his fasting and penance, Arjuna was a Kshatriya still, and the hot blood of the Kshatriya which flowed in his veins would not be subdued. He would never refuse a challenge to fight.

So they strung their bows and the arrows began to fly. But though a hundred arrows pierced Arjuna's body till the blood ran down his limbs in great streams, Arjuna's arrows did not so much as touch the hunter. Instead they fell at his feet as if they had been flowers. After a while, Arjuna's quiver was empty and he had no more arrows to shoot. Then he rushed at his adversary with his bow, but the hunter wrenched it away from him without effort, as if it had been a toy. Arjuna drew his sword, but the sword broke and fell from his hand.

So they fell to wrestling. Once again the tribesman proved invincible, for Arjuna was scarcely able even to touch him. On the other hand, the hunter again and again brought him to the earth. But as many times as he was knocked down, so many times did Arjuna spring up, refusing to acknowledge defeat. There was no part of him that was not injured. His bones were like pulp inside his battered body. Blood flowed from it and soaked the earth where they stood. Still Arjuna would not stop. Still he fought on.

Then at last came his darkest hour, when he was thrown upon the ground and had not the strength even to get up. At that moment Arjuna remembered his God and surrendered himself completely to him, praying humbly and desperately for help. Finding a garland of flowers near him, he threw it upon the clay image of Mahadeva, but even as he watched, they were transposed to the neck of the hunter. Arjuna stared at the marvellous occurrence and realized with a strange sense of awakening that this was no forest hunter at all, but Mahadeva himself. Then Arjuna cried out in joy and crept up to the tribesman's feet, begging forgiveness. Mahadeva smiled and raised him up; at his touch the strength flowed back into Arjuna's body, his wounds healed, his skin grew smooth and he became whole again.

Mahadeva, who was pleased with Arjuna's valour, gave to him the weapons which he had prayed for, and blessed him, declaring that final victory would be on his side; and after the great God had blessed him there appeared before Arjuna the lesser gods, who also gave

him their weapons—Yama his noose, Kubera
his arrows of sleep, and Varuna his mace. Over-
helmed by the kindness of the gods, Arjuna
struggled in vain to find words to thank them.
But they understood his gratitude and smiled
and vanished from his presence, leaving him
standing there alone, with their wonderful gifts
around him. Then Indra, the King of the gods,
returned and took Arjuna to his kingdom in the
heavens in his winged chariot. Here Arjuna
lived in comfort for five years, learning the use
of the weapons he had won and many other
sciences and arts, and even music and dance
from Chitrasena, the heavenly musician of Indra.
Arjuna proved an apt pupil and it was not long
before he became an accomplished artist. When
he felt he had learnt all the things that had to
be learned, Indra sent him back to the earth
with his blessing, promising him and his brothers
victory over their enemies.

*   *   *   *   *

Another time, it happened that the Pandava
brothers, going in pursuit of a deer in the forest,
wandered far from their dwelling place. The sun
was hot overhead and they grew thirsty. The

deer had vanished, and now footsore and weary
they came at last to a st?, knowing that their
search was in vain. Th? mouths were parched;
they scanned the e?? in all directions for some
sign of water. ?t seeing none, they trudged
wearily onwa? until at last Yudhishthira, unable for hi? atigue to go any further, sank down
under a ?ee to rest and sent Sahadeva in search
of w?er for them. The youth went readily
en?gh, but when he did not return for a long
?ime, Yudhishthira grew concerned. He sent
Nakula to see what had happened and also to
find water. Nakula obeyed—but he too, like
Sahadeva, did not return. Then one by one
Yudhishthira sent his brothers after each other,
but when they all went and none returned he
grew very anxious, not knowing what evil fate
had overtaken them. At last he decided to go
and see for himself; he got up and following in
their footsteps, went down the track. He walked
down for a distance until he came to a pool in a
clearing in the forest. Its clear, still waters reflected the blue sky while the pink and white
and blue lotuses that grew in it raised their
smiling heads to the sun. But as his eyes looked
upon the lovely scene, Yudhishthira saw another
sight that made his blood freeze in his veins.

For upon the ea.. lay his four brothers, cold and still, either dead . unconscious. Their eyes were closed and whe. he called to them they would not answer. Sorrow .lled the king's heart, and he fell on his knees b. them and wept bitterly for them, wringing h. hands in his grief and crying out to heaven to .ke him too, for he could not live without his bro.ers.

Now though Yudhishthira did not .ow it, this was what had happened: One by one his brothers had come to this forest pool. T.e first to come was Sahadeva. He was full of joy at seeing water, for he was very thirsty. He knelt upon the bank and bent down to drink of the waters of the pool when a voice broke through the silence of the grove. "Stop Sahadeva!" said the voice, "Do not drink, for this is an enchanted pool." Startled, Sahadeva looked about him, but he could see no one. He turned to the water. It looked cool and inviting. He was very thirsty. As he paused, undecided, the voice rang out again:—

"I am a Yaksha," it said "and, this enchanted pool belongs to me. No one may drink of its water until he has answered my questions."

Sahadeva rose up and waited.

He could still see nobody. He seemed to be

alone except for the birds chirping in the trees and the dragon flies zooming over the water.

"It must be my fancy," Sahadeva thought, "The hot sun makes my imagination work."

He decided to ignore the voice of the invisible speaker. He was too tired and thirsty to wait. He made a cup of his hands and kneeling down began to drink. But hardly had the water touched his lips, when he felt himself struck down. Sahadeva's senses reeled. The world went dark and he fell down unconscious.

When Nakula arrived shortly afterwards he was grieved and surprised to see his brother in this condition. But so great was his own thirst that he did not wait. He rushed to the water's edge to drink. But as he stooped, he too heard the Yaksha's warning voice. However, he too paid no attention. He drank and instantly he too was struck down and rendered unconscious. When Bhima came to the spot, the same fate overtook him, though he was strong and mighty, and though he sent a shower of arrows in all directions and searched all round for the hidden enemy.

Arjuna fared no better, and when Yudhishthira came at last to the pool in search of them he found his four brothers lying as if they were dead. For a long time Yudhishthira wept over them. Then, feeling his thirst overpower him, he dragged himself to the edge of the water. But as he bent down, Yushishthira heard the Yaksha's warning voice. Yudhishthira looked around. "Who are you?" he asked. "Ask your questions and I shall answer them as well as I can."

Then the voice said: "I am a Yaksha, O Yudhishthira, and it is well for you that you heeded my warning. Now listen to my questions."

"What makes the sun shine?"

"The power of God!" Yudhishthira answered.

"What is man's surest weapon against danger?" the Yaksha asked, and Yudhishthira said, "Courage! Courage is his surest weapon in danger."

"What gives more to man than even the earth does? What feeds him and sustains him and makes him strong?" the Yaksha questioned. Yudhishthira replied, "A mother, surely. It is only a mother who gives a man life and feeds him and sustains him. A mother is more than the earth."

"When does a man become loved by his fellows?" asked the Yaksha, and Yudhishthira returned, "When he gives up pride." "What is that which makes a man happy when he has lost it?" the Yaksha went on. "Anger," said

Yudhishthira, without hesitation, for he knew that when a man gives up anger, then he is full of peace. The Yaksha continued:

"What can a man give up and immediately become rich?"

"Desire," answered Yudhishthira, "It is only the man without desires who is really rich; but even if a man has a thousand things he will be poor if he is not satisfied." So the Yaksha asked his questions, and Yudhishthira answered them until at last the Yaksha said, "O king, I am well pleased with your answers, and I shall restore to you one of your brothers. Choose who it shall be."

Yudhishthira looked at the unconscious forms of his brothers. It was hard for him to decide. But he spoke at last:

"O kind Yaksha," he said "Restore to me my brother Nakula." "And why Nakula?" the Yaksha's voice asked. "Is not Bhima more useful to you? Will you not benefit from his great strength in the war that will surely come? And Arjuna—why do you not choose Arjuna? Is he not dearer to you than all? Is he not the most handsome, the most skilled among them all in the use of arms? Why then do you choose Nakula?"

Then Yudhishthira gave his noblest answer—
"Listen, O Yaksha," he said. "Righteousness
and truth are a man's only weapon and protec-
tion. The strength of Bhima and the skill of
Arjuna would be of no use to me if I acted
unrighteously. Indeed I would be unrighteous
if I looked to my own gain and begged for
Bhima's life or Arjuna's in preference to Nakula's.
For Nakula is Madri's son, and Bhima and
Arjuna, like me, are Kunti's children. Of Kunti's
children I at least live. But if Nakula and
Sahadeva should both die, then Madri's line
would end. Therefore, O Yaksha, it is right that
Nakula's life should be restored rather than
Bhima's or Arjuna's."

When he had said this a wonderful thing
happened. In a moment there appeared before
Yudhishthira a shining, crowned person whom
he knew at once to be a god, and no human
being at all. Yudhishthira was right. The strange
personage was no other than Yama, god of
Justice and Death, Yudhishthira's heavenly
father. Yama embraced Yudhishthira and told
him who he was, and how he had come to help
the Pandavas in their hour of need. He told him
how pleased he was with Yudhishthira's noble
conduct and wisdom, and he restored to life

not just one of the brothers, but all of them. They arose and looked about them, dazed and unable to understand what had happened.

But Yudhishthira knelt at his heavenly father's feet and his heart overflowed with gratitude. Yama blessed him and promised that he and his brothers would be protected by heaven in their hardships.

"No harm shall come to you," he said. "Neither will you be discovered while you live in hiding during the last and thirteenth year of exile."

He advised Yudhishthira to go with his brothers and Draupadi to Matsya, where the good king Virata ruled, and to live there in disguise. There they would be safe from their enemies while they awaited the end of their long period of exile.

Then Yama left Yudhishthira, who returned to his forest dwelling with his brothers.

CHAPTER XXII

THE PANDAVAS COME TO MATSYA, AND KICHAKA MEETS HIS DEATH

HE Pandavas spent the last year of their exile in Matsya, the kingdom of the good king Virata, as Yama had advised them to do. According to the terms of the agreement with Duryodhana, they must disguise themselves and remain in hiding for a year. If they were discovered they would have to remain in exile and serve yet another twelve-year period in the forest. The Pandavas were certainly not anxious to repeat their sentence. They held anxious consultations together about the disguise each was to take.

Yudhishthira declared that he would go into Matsya dressed as a courtier, a nobleman who had seen better days but who, through misfortune had lost all his wealth and fallen from his high estate. He would be companion to King Virata, amusing him with his conversation and playing games of dice with him.

Bhima said that he would go disguised as a cook to work in Virata's royal kitchens.

Nakula told his brothers that he would work in Virata's stables among his horses, and Sahadeva, his twin, asked to be allowed to go as herdsman who would have the care of Virata's large herds of cattle. Arjuna, who had learnt music and dancing from Chitrasena at Indra's court, decided to disguise himself as a teacher of music and dancing. He would teach these arts to the King's children. He would remain in the women's apartments dressed like a woman, the battle scars upon his rough hard hands hidden under bangles and ornaments. A strange mannish woman he would seem—gruff-voiced, tall and ungainly. Perhaps they would laugh and poke fun at him. But he would go about his work cleverly and he would not be discovered.

Then Draupadi spoke. "I will go as Queen Sudeshana's serving-maiden and companion," she said, and Yudhishthira hung his head in shame as he heard her and his eyes filled with tears, remembering how all her life Draupadi had been brought up in comfort and luxury. As her husband he had vowed to protect her and look after her. Yudhishthira knew he had failed his wife. He saw now, as he had never done before, where his folly had led them. But Draupadi begged him to take heart and Yudhishthira knew there was no other way. Heavy-hearted and full of shame he had to agree to Draupadi's proposal.

Then the Pandavas sent to King Drupada's court their lamps and idols of worship, and said goodbye to Dhaumya their priest, who had been with them during their twelve years in the forest. Collecting their arms and weapons in a bundle, they brought them at midnight to a cremation ground where the people burned their dead. Here, moving softly and stealthily, they hung the bundle upon the topmost branches of a tall tree. Then each disguised himself and silently, one after another, taking different paths, they left the forest.

King Virata of Matsya was a good and kindly man who harmed no one. He honoured the gods and tried to live according to the law. But without strength of mind or character, he proved a weak ruler. Though he sat upon the throne of Matsya, real power lay in the hands of Kichaka, his brother-in-law, Queen Sudeshana's brother who lived in the royal palace. Now Kichaka was a greedy, cruel man, but he was also strong and brave. People feared him, and he kept law and order in the country. The neighbouring people dared not make trouble upon Matsya's borders, for if they did Kichaka would come down on them with a heavy hand. So they kept their hands off Virata's territory and respected its boundaries.

The five Pandava brothers came into Matsya to King Virata, not all together but one by one, as if each did not know the other. The kindly Virata employed each one in his service; Yudhishthira as a companion to him, a courtier who could amuse him and play games with him; Bhima as royal cook; Arjuna as a teacher of dance and music; Nakula and Sahadeva respectively as syce and herdsman.

Then Draupadi came before Queen Sudeshana and begged to be employed by her as companion and serving-maiden. Queen Sudeshana was pleased with the young woman's noble bearing and appearance. She wondered who she was. Draupadi told her that she was the wife of five gods who lived in the heavens and watched over her and protected her constantly. She told her that once long ago, she had served Queen Draupadi at Indraprashtha, but when evil days had fallen upon the Pandavas she had had to leave Indraprashtha to seek employment elsewhere. Draupadi also told Queen Sudeshana that she would work for her only on one condition: she would serve no one but the queen or the king. Greatly struck by the serving woman's manner and good looks, Sudeshana agreed to her condition and employed her.

So Draupadi and the Pandavas lived and worked unrecognized at Virata's royal court. They moved about with care, watching their actions and their words to make sure they would not be discovered and they gave no sign to anyone that they knew each other.

It was not easy for them, however, to live as lowly servants taking orders from others, where they had always commanded; but they bore their lot without complaining. This last year which they must spend in hiding was perhaps the hardest of all, but they felt that the end of their troubles was now in sight. Remembering this, they took courage.

Thus ten months went by, and they rejoiced that nobody suspected their identity. Then an unfortunate incident took place which nearly brought them to ruin:

It happened one day that Kichaka's eyes fell on Draupadi, who worked as his sister's serving-maiden under the name of Sairandhri. He was infatuated with her beauty and wanted to have her as his slave. But Draupadi would have none of him, and fled from his unwelcome attentions. Kichaka who was used to having his own way in everything came to his sister and asked for her beautiful serving-maiden. Queen Sudeshana demurred,[1] pointing out to him that as the woman did not care to go to him it would not be right to force her.

Kichaka however did not think that a slave's feelings mattered in the least. And Sudeshana, who was fond of her brother, gave in to him.

That evening Sudeshana commanded Draupadi to go with a goblet of wine to Kichaka's house. Draupadi's entreaties to be excused from the hateful task, her tears reminding her that she had agreed to serve only the king and queen, her threats about the anger of her invisible husbands, all fell on deaf ears. Sudeshana would not be crossed.

She thrust the goblet into Draupadi's hands and commanded her to go, her haughty face dark with anger. Draupadi, however, had no intention of becoming Kichaka's slave. She took the goblet to Kichaka's house but would

[1] hesitated, objected.

not enter its doorway. She saw him at the entrance and thrusting it quickly into his hands she fled. Thwarted and taken by surprise Kichaka ran after her, calling her to stop. But Draupadi continued to run until she reached the pleasure hall where King Virata sat playing dice with Yudhishthira. With a cry she flung herself at the King's feet, begging him to protect her.

Kichaka was not far behind. The next instant he came up. He had no regard for king or court. His anger had been aroused and his pride had been wounded. Before Virata could say anything he kicked Draupadi where she knelt.

No one else moved. No one dared to rise—neither the king nor the nobles, nor even Yudhishthira, for they all feared Kichaka too much to pay attention to the insult to a serving-maiden. Yudhishthira, of course, had his own reasons for not coming to Draupadi's help. He knew that he must give no sign that he knew Draupadi or that she meant anything to him, for if he did, they might all be discovered before their time. Duryodhana's spies were everywhere and one could not be too careful. So though his heart ached for his wife, Yudhishthira too remained silent like the others.

When he saw how they all feared him, Kichaka

laughed aloud, proud and satisfied, and strode away. After a while poor Draupadi crept away, weeping, to her quarters.

That night, when everyone was asleep, Draupadi tip-toed out of her room and made her way into the servants' quarters where Bhima slept. She shook him and whispering his name softly, woke him. Then she beckoned to him and led him to a secret place where weeping hot, bitter tears, she poured out to him the story of the day's happenings, and begged him to avenge the insult she had suffered. Hearing her, Bhima, who loved her more than his life, ground his teeth in anger.

"Kill Kichaka if you have any love for me!" she cried out, "or if you will not kill him, say so, and I will kill myself. This disgrace is more than I can bear." Bhima nodded grimly: "Kichaka shall not live," he promised her. His words comforted Draupadi.

Bhima laid his plans carefully, for he knew that if they were discovered before their time they would have played into Duryodhana's hands.

He told Draupadi that she must go to Kichaka and appear to be sorry for what she had done. She must pretend to feel love for him and entice him cleverly into the dancing hall at dead of night. There he would get what he deserved.

Draupadi agreed to do all he said.

She went about her part of the plot calmly. When Kichaka swaggered up to her the next day she sidled towards him, pretending to admire him. Kichaka, who was as vain and conceited as he was stupid, smirked delightedly and fell headlong into the snare. Draupadi flattered him and spoke sweetly to him until she made him promise to meet her secretly in the dance hall that same night. And Kichaka went away, little knowing what was in store for him.

"Now you are properly fixed!" thought Draupadi grimly as she watched him go. "It is lucky that your wits do not match your strength!"

That night Kichaka met his death. For when he came to the dance hall, he saw a muffled figure on a couch. Believing it was Sairandhri he went close and called her name. Kichaka never knew what happened next, for it all happened so swiftly. The figure arose and cast off the cloak. The next minute he was caught in arms, stronger, it seemed, than iron. He was still struggling to get free when a sharp, swift blow on his face sent him reeling to the floor, and a heavy form was upon him, gagging his mouth and strangling his throat.

Quickly recovering his presence of mind, Kichaka struggled to rise. Whatever his faults, he lacked neither strength nor courage. But Bhima would not let go his hold. He fell upon him and pounded his head mercilessly till the blood flowed.

When he was sure Kichaka was dead, Bhima got up and slipped away as noiselessly as he had come. He returned to the servants' quarters where he washed his blood-stained hands. Then quietly he returned to bed.

The next morning the palace was astir with the news of the murder of Kichaka. An unknown enemy had made short work of the mighty commander-in-chief of the Matsyan army, whom all men had feared because of his great strength and power. People whispered in fear, not knowing what to think. Queen Sudeshana mourned for her brother and looked darkly at 'Sairandhri'. In her heart she felt sure that this mysterious woman had something to do with his death. But when she questioned her, Draupadi answered sullenly: "How should I know? Did I not warn you that my invisible husbands are strong and

Bhima fell upon him and pounded his head
mercilessly.

jealous?" Queen Sudeshana would have dismissed her from service, but Draupadi reminded her that according to the conditions of her service, she had been appointed for a year and could not be turned away before that time. So Draupadi remained.

There was mourning and grief in Matsya for Kichaka. He had been a cruel tyrant and an arrogant man, but he had kept Matsya strong and had protected her from enemy attack. Now that his strong hands had been removed, people feared that Matsya's neighbours would start their mischievous activities again, raiding her border villages, stealing her cattle and crops and terrorising her people. Perhaps there would be an invasion and war. There was trouble in store now, and no one to stand at the helm of affairs and lead the people.

CHAPTER XXIII

DURYODHANA'S ATTACK ON MATSYA

THE fears of the Matsya people were not groundless, for even as they were mourning the death of their commander-in-chief, enemies who had been waiting and watching for an opportunity rose up again and began to bestir themselves with preparations to attack the defenceless country.

Among these enemies were Susharma, King of Trigarta, and Duryodhana, ruler of Hastinapura. Duryodhana had not dared to attack Matsya when Kichaka was alive.

But when he heard the news of Kichaka's death, he went over the details in his mind again: A mysterious person, they said, had killed Kichaka—an invisible Gandharva, reported to be one of the five husbands of a beautiful and proud serving-maiden, Sairandhri.

Duryodhana frowned to himself. It all seemed to fit so well. He felt sure that the mysterious killer of Kichaka was no other than Bhima, for it was known that in all the world there was only Bhima who could equal Kichaka in strength.

Duryodhana's mind began to work busily away as he hatched his plan. When he had worked out all the details he announced his intentions to the elders.

"I do not think the Pandavas are dead," he told them. "I think they are living in Matsya and that the killer of Kichaka is no other than Bhima."

"However," he went on, "whether the Pandavas live there or not, one thing is certain: Kichaka, defender of Matsya, is dead. Now is the time to strike at Virata's kingdom, before he has time to recover and build up his strength. Virata will never be able to withstand us alone. Let us therefore attack Matsya and carry away her cattle."

His eyes gleamed as he continued: "If Virata has given shelter to the Pandavas, then they will surely give him help and fight for him. Then of course they will be discovered before their time and that will be their doom. Either way we stand to gain by making war."

A roar of acclamation greeted Duryodhana's words. It came from Susharma and Karna, who cried out for war, brandishing their shining weapons and twanging their bow strings till the assembly hall resounded with the noise.

The voices that pleaded for peace, for restraint, for caution were drowned that day in the clamour for war. War was what Duryodhana and his friends wanted, and this time they had their way. It was agreed in the council that met soon afterwards that Susharma should attack Matsya on her southern frontiers and engage her armies in battle, while Karna and Duryodhana would launch a surprise attack on the north.

In accordance with this plan, Susharma's armies struck Matsya in the south and began to lay the countryside waste and harass the people. As they began to make their way towards the capital, the people panicked, defenceless as they were against the marauding soldiers. They sent messengers to the king with appeals for help.

The messengers arriving at the palace found Virata in the dice room playing a game with his favourite courtier Kanka—who was really Yudhishthira, and they cried out to him to come and save them from the plundering armies.

Virata listened to their tale of woe. "Now our troubles have started," he thought, "and I am not strong enough to lead the country

against the invaders." He wished Kichaka had
been alive, and said so to his companion.
"Kichaka was headstrong and often wicked in
his ways," he said, "but he was strong. As long
as he was alive no one dared to touch our
frontiers."

Yudhishthira answered him, "Sir, you do
not need to fear. Indeed we cannot waste time
thinking over what might have been. Now is
the time for action."

"I do not feel equal to it," Virata protested
weakly. "I am a peace-loving man. I like to be
left alone."

Yudhishthira cut him short, "This is not the
time for talk or for explanations," he said
briskly. "Now we must act. You must get your
army together and march upon the enemy."

"How?" cried Virata frantically. "Susharma
is strong!"

"Listen!" said Yudhishthira, "I will help you.
I have been in the service of the Pandavas in
Indraprastha and I know the art of warfare.
Besides, there are others. There is Balala your
cook and there are Dharmagranti, who is in
charge of your horses, and Tantripala who
looks after your cattle. They too have been, like
me, in the service of the Pandavas. They will

come to your aid. Appoint them officers in
your forces. Give them power and authority
and they will drive out the invaders."

Virata was too distracted and frightened to
argue. He was willing to give over charge to
any one who would take it. He did as he was
told, and Balala, who was really Bhima, and
Dharmagranti and Tantripala, who were really
Nakula and Sahadeva, were quickly sent for
and given charge of army units. Yudhishthira
was placed at the head of the forces and Virata
as King rode in his chariot beside him.

Thus the Matsya forces came out to fight
the invaders. Nobody knew who the mysterious
military commanders were. But whoever they
were they proved their valour and skill on the
battlefield that day. The armies of Susharma
fled before them like chaff in the wind. But
when they re-grouped and in a sudden surprise
attack captured Virata the tide seemed to turn
against the Matsyan forces; then Balala riding
into the thick of battle, and piercing through
the enemy formations, rescued him from the
jaws of death and brought him to safety.
Susharma's soldiers fled in confusion.

The news of the victory spread as if on wings.
The people went wild with joy and began to

make preparations for Virata's triumphal return to the capital. Everywhere there was rejoicing in which the recent misfortunes were forgotten.

And now, when the citizens were making merry, Duryodhana struck at Matsya's northern frontiers and advanced upon the unsuspecting people. As Susharma had done in the south, so the Kaurava armies did in the north, plundering, looting and laying the countryside waste. And, as before so now once more messengers came flying to the capital to beg the king for help.

But the king was away and all the citizens were busy with preparations for his triumphal entry after his victory. The capital was deserted and there was not one to whom the messengers could speak, except the young prince Uttara Kumar, Virata's son and heir to his throne.

Uttara Kumar was in the women's apartments with his mother and other ladies when they came. He was a young lad, hardly more than a child, and the ladies of the court loved him and petted and spoilt him incessantly.

When the messengers were brought before him he listened carefully to them: "There is no one who can help us now, O Prince," they cried, "except you."

Uttara Kumar flushed with pride and his

eyes sparkled. "I will lead the people," he answered, full of boyish enthusiasm. The ladies laughed delightedly and applauded him, charmed with his ways. And Sudeshana's heart went out to him in motherly pride.

Only Sairandhri said, "You will no doubt win the war, O Prince, but before you go, I would request you to take with you Brihanalla, the dancing teacher. She will prove a useful companion, for it is said that she is skilled in the charioteer's art."

Prince Uttara pouted a little. "Whoever heard of a woman on a battle-field?" he protested; but Sairandhri answered firmly, "She will be useful to you, O Prince, for she is skilled at chariot-driving and you have no chariot driver."

So at last Prince Uttara was persuaded and Brihanalla (who was really Arjuna in disguise) was given armour to wear and a whip to hold. Then, bidding the ladies good-bye, the young prince and his companion mounted the chariot.

Brihanalla cracked the whip and shouted to the horses and away they sped northwards to face the Kaurava army.

CHAPTER XXIV

PRINCE UTTARA KUMAR GOES INTO BATTLE

RIHANALLA proved a skilled charioteer, much to the young Prince's surprise. They sped swiftly over the countryside and Uttara Kumar chattered to him freely, boasting in boyish fashion about what he would do upon the battle-field. But when on the third day they sighted the Kaurava army in the distance, when they heard the war cries of the soldiers and the dreadful clamour of arms, the twanging of bow-strings, the rattling of sabres and the blare of conch shells, when he saw the fierce ruddy faces of the warriors, Prince Uttara Kumar lost heart and began to tremble. For he was young and inexperienced, and had never before left the shelter of his home in the palace. He clung to Arjuna begging him piteously to take him back home, and all Arjuna's attempts to encourage him were of no avail. "They will jeer at you if you return now!" he said. "Even the ladies will laugh."

"Let them laugh!" cried the Prince, hiding his face in his hands. "I cannot fight the Kauravas."

Arjuna would not let him give way to his fear in this manner. "You must take hold of yourself," he said. "You cannot behave like a woman."

"I cannot help it," sobbed the Prince. "Take me back, O Brihanalla. Take me back, I implore you."

Arjuna tried again: "I will give you weapons," he promised him, "weapons like those the Pandavas used."

Uttara Kumar struggled in his grasp. "I do not want weapons," he cried, "I want to go home. Take me to my mother."

"I will do no such thing," Arjuna answered him firmly. "You are a Kshatriya; you have warrior blood in you. Your duty is to fight for your people and country. I will give you weapons such as you have never seen in all your life. Only take heart."

And he turned a deaf ear to the poor boy's entreaties. He caught Uttara Kumar's hands and tied him to the chariot so that he could not escape.

Then ignoring the boy's cries he steered the

224

He caught Uttar Kumar's hands.

chariot to that lonely cremation ground where earlier that year, he and his brothers had put their weapons in a bundle and hung them up on a tree.

"Look!" he pointed out to the Prince. "Do you see that object hanging from the tree?"

"It is a corpse," the terrified Prince screamed. "Why have you brought me to this fearsome place, haunt of evil spirits? Take me back!"

"Listen," said Arjuna, paying no heed to his cries. "In that bundle are the weapons of the Pandavas. Climb the tree and get the bundle down."

His voice was so stern, so commanding, that Uttara dared not disobey. Trembling, he climbed the tree and got the bundle down.

"Untie the knots," the charioteer went on in the same stern note. Uttara Kumar obeyed. When he did so he found inside the shining weapons the charioteer had promised.

"These weapons belong to the Pandavas," said the charioteer, and seeing them the Prince felt his heart lift with new hope. He turned to the charioteer.

"Who are you?" he asked huskily. "Surely you are no humble dancing teacher! Surely you are no charioteer! Tell me who you are "

Prince Uttara Kumar goes into Battle

Then Arjuna revealed himself to the youth, who thrilled to see him and felt courage surge through him again; for he knew that victory was certain now with the great hero to fight on his side. He knelt down before the warrior with deep humility and reverence. But Arjuna raised him up and embraced him. He spoke to him stirring words, reminding him of his great heritage as a Kshatriya. Hearing them the boy took heart. He climbed back into the chariot and together the two went into battle.

From afar the Kauravas saw the chariot in which Prince Uttara Kumar rode with Arjuna, and Duryodhana, seeing the boy riding into battle with no better companion than a mannish-looking woman, was completely confident of victory. But even as he was crowing over his chances and chuckling to himself, the fearful sound of the twanging of Arjuna's bowstring filled the air and its resonance seemed to reach the very heavens.

Hearing it, the Kauravas exchanged looks in silence. They each knew that terrible sound and they recognized it now. For there was no sound in all the world like that of Arjuna's bowstring.

Slowly they began to voice their doubts; at that moment, three swift arrows came speeding through the air and fell, one at Bhishma's feet, one at Drona's and the third at Kripa's. The elders looked at each other and nodded, and Drona announced: "It is just as I had thought; Arjuna stands on the other side of the field. These arrows are proof of the truth of my guess, for with these arrows Arjuna sends his salutations to his elders and teachers. We must move with care."

Drona's words of caution angered Karna, who felt that Drona's heart was not in the fight. It seemed to Karna that Drona was counselling them in this way because he loved the Pandavas. Karna taunted Drona and charged him with disloyalty to the Kauravas; and Ashwathama, Drona's son, stung by the taunts, answered him back sharply. Duryodhana joined the wordy duel on Karna's side: "What does it matter even if it should be Arjuna?" he said to Drona. "According to the terms of the wager the Pandavas agreed to return to the forest to serve another twelve year period of exile if they were discovered before their time. Arjuna has been discovered and the Pandavas will have to pay for his bravado by returning into exile!"

But while Duryodhana was speaking Drona had been calculating rapidly in his mind.

"According to the movements of the heavenly bodies, the thirteen years ended at the very moment we heard the sound of the bowstring, O Duryodhana!" he answered. "The Pandavas have fulfilled the terms of their pledge!"

His words made Duryodhana furious: "Karna is right!" he shouted. "Your heart is with the Pandavas. You are a traitor."

Ashwathama sprang to his father's side and drew his sword, but Drona held him back. "Mind your words, Duryodhana!" he warned, "Mind your words!"

Karna stood by Duryodhana. "Why else does he always speak in their favour?" he questioned angrily. "Why does he not prove his loyalty to us by his deeds?"

Thus hot words were flung at each other, and even before the battle had started there was a rift in the Kaurava camp. But while they squabbled together, Bhishma came up and spoke sternly to them, reminding them that this was not the time for them to quarrel over petty issues. "Now we must close our ranks and come together, for we are standing on a battle-field," said Bhishma.

The quarrel was patched up for a while, but the angers and suspicions that had caused it remained.

The battle that followed was a short but decisive one. Arjuna's arrows sped in all directions so swiftly that the Kauravas could not advance. They had not counted on such a fierce adversary. Taken completely by surprise they retreated in confusion, broke cover and fled. Duryodhana, driving before him the cattle they had stolen, found himself pursued hotly and forced to give up all he had—the cattle, his weapons, even the very clothes that he wore! The other Kauravas fared no better. It was a complete and crushing defeat.

A broken and dispirited army made its way back to Hastinapura at the end of the battle, humiliated and in disgrace.

CHAPTER XXV

THE PANDAVAS MAKE THEMSELVES KNOWN

RJUNA and Uttara Kumar had won a great victory. They turned back to return to the capital. But the glad news of their triumph had gone before them. Crowds of people thronged the streets to greet them as they came. Conch shells boomed and drums throbbed. Everywhere they received a hero's welcome.

In the palace King Virata was beside himself with joy. He gave orders for a great welcome to be prepared for the Prince. He talked about his son incessantly, bragging about him in his fatherly pride, especially to Kanka, his favourite courtier.

Now Kanka, who was really Yudhishthira, had always echoed the King's sentiments. During the one year that he had been in Virata's service he had never displeased him by expressing any opinion that was contrary to his. Virata was therefore surprised when Kanka did not respond with his usual enthusiasm. The truth was that Yudhishthira had made up his mind to reveal his identity, now that the period of exile had ended. But Virata did not know this. Each time Virata spoke in praise of his son's courage and heroism the courtier, instead of assenting enthusiastically and echoing his words, as the King expected him to do, answered in a very different tone. He referred time and again very pointedly to Brihanalla's part in the battle, declaring with a little smile that but for Brihanalla the victory would not have been possible. King Virata was greatly annoyed. He felt that Kanka was belittling his son's part in the battle, and he could not believe that the victory was won by a woman. Virata wondered if this courtier was not over-reaching himself and growing rather insolent. He decided to ignore Kanka's remarks, but when the latter repeated them several times making his meaning quite clear, Virata lost patience. They were sitting at their usual game of dice and Virata, suddenly angered, flung the dice at Yudhishthira's cheek so hard that it cut him and the blood began to trickle down.

At that moment Draupadi was in the room. Seeing the blood she gave a little cry of distress and hurried to her husband's side. With a silken cloth she wiped the blood and squeezed it out into a cup of gold.

"Why, what a fuss!" cried Virata impatiently. "What foolishness is this, woman? Why do you collect the blood in a golden cup?"

"Because he is a King, O Virata," Draupadi answered, "and royal blood must not fall upon the earth. If it does it will be evil for the land. There will be famine and pestilence and sorrow. Have you not heard this saying, O Virata?"

"A King!" Virata cried out puzzled. "What King?" He was finding it hard to control his anger. He could not understand anything.

At that minute the door burst open and with a loud joyful cry the young prince Uttara Kumar entered and fell at his father's feet. Virata raised him up, all other things forgotten in his happiness at seeing his son returned from the field of battle.

"My valiant boy!" Virata exclaimed, "You have proved your worth today, defeating the most powerful princes in the land...."

But Uttara Kumar interrupted him "O, Father!" he said, "it was not my doing at all. See, here is the one who led us to victory."

"Brihanalla, the dance teacher!" Virata uttered, completely stupefied.

Prince Uttara Kumar said in a husky voice, full of reverence, "Father, this is no dance teacher, though for a year he lived among us as such. This is Arjuna, the Pandava returned from exile!" and he told his father the story. Virata's amazement was equalled only by his great joy. His eyes filled with happy tears.

"Arjuna!" he repeated again and again. "It is as if you have returned from the dead."

Then suddenly he spied Yudhishthira and Draupadi. Her words came back to his mind. "He is a King, and royal blood must not be allowed to soak the earth." In a flash he understood it all. He went up to Yudhishthira and, standing before him with folded hands, humbly begged forgiveness for all the harsh words he had unknowingly spoken to him.

But Yudhishthira bore Virata no ill-will. He embraced Virata warmly. "You have given us shelter in your kingdom, O Virata, my brother," he said, "we who were homeless and pursued by powerful enemies. How can I hold anything against you?"

Then Virata led Yudhishthira to the throne, and Sudeshana, the queen, came forward and begged Draupadi to forgive the many wrongs she had done her. King Virata did the Pandavas

great honour, so full he was of gratitude to them
for having helped him against powerful enemies
that day.

To show his gratitude he led his daughter,
the princess Uttara, to Arjuna and begged him
to accept her as his bride. But this Arjuna would
not consent to do. "She is only a child," he said,
"and I am no longer young. While I have lived
here I have looked upon her as my daughter."

He put his hand upon the girl's head. "One
day, there will come one worthier of this pure
and gentle creature than an old battle-scarred
warrior like me." Arjuna was thinking of his
young son Abhimanyu, son of Subadhra.

During the days that followed there was
feasting and merry-making in Matsya to cele-
brate the victories and welcome the Pandavas.
Virata sent invitations to all the friends and
kinsmen of the Pandavas to come and greet
them after their long sojourn in the forest. They
came, borne upon their golden palanquins
and riding their chariots, bringing with them
presents and tribute and tokens of good will.
Among them were Drupada of Panchala and
Krishna and Balarama of Dwaraka. With
Drupada came his sons and grandsons, children
of Draupadi, while Krishna brought with him

his sister Subadhra, Arjuna's wife, and her son Abhimanyu.

When Arjuna saw his son, his heart swelled with love and pride to see how he had grown. For he was tall and handsome, his eyes bright and clear, his brow noble and good. He held himself straight and stepped forward with such grace and modesty and such princely dignity that tears rose in Arjuna's throat and filled his eyes. He pressed him to his bosom, unable to speak for the fullness of his heart. And then Arjuna thought of Uttara, Virata's daughter. It seemed to Arjuna that heaven had made these children for each other. He spoke his thought to Virata and the latter was delighted with the proposal.

Soon preparations were afoot for the marriage of Abhimanyu to Uttara. The news was carried by drummers to the furthest corners of the land and the people went mad with joy. There was music and dancing and the gaily decorated streets were crowded with revellers. The marriage of Uttara and Abhimanyu was celebrated with great pomp and splendour. Everywhere there was laughter and merry-making, and outside the palace people waited by thousands to see the youthful couple.

The Pandavas Make Themselves Known

Oh, the sun shone brightly that day from unclouded skies and it was the season of joy and love and laughter! For a while men forgot their sorrows and hatreds and put aside their doubts and misgivings and wished the young couple happiness and long life.

As for Abhimanyu and Uttara, they were well pleased with each other. Each looked into the other's eyes and saw there a deep and loving tenderness. Bitter days were to follow and their young lives were to be clouded over with grief and tragedy. Violence and treachery and death were to cut the slender, slender thread of their happiness, and sorrow and tears were to be the lot of the sweet young Uttara, who never in her life hurt another by look or word or deed. But the future was hidden from them, and now they stood together, hand in hand, on the threshold of a new life and their young, innocent hearts were happy.

CHAPTER XXVI

THE PANDAVAS AND THEIR ALLIES
CONFER TOGETHER

T THE end of the marriage festivities Abhimanyu led his sweet young bride before each of the persons assembled there, and the two bent low to touch their feet and receive their blessings. The elders, touched by their youth and innocence, wished them well and blessed them. Then the young couple retired into the inner apartments, to the courtyards of the palace where silver fountains played and rainbow-coloured fish swam in marble pools. They wandered among the flower-beds, and spoke and laughed and were happy together.

But in the court-room where the Pandavas and Virata and their allies had assembled, the atmosphere was very different indeed. For the men who had gathered here were hardened warriors and men of the world, grave, troubled men, weighed down by many fears and anxieties.

238

Pandavas and their allies confer together.

The matters they had assembled to discuss
related, of course, to the return of the Pandavas
to their old position. The Pandavas had redeemed the pledge they had made to their
cousins. What were they to do next? How
should they set about their task? Should they
go before Duryodhana and demand from him
the kingdom he had wrested from them by
such foul means? Or should they go humbly
on bended knees and take what he chose to
give?

How much of their territory should they claim?
What if Duryodhana refused to acknowledge
their rights and to restore to them their kingdom
and belongings? What course were they to take
in that case? The Pandavas and their friends
knew that Duryodhana would not easily part
with his unlawful gains.

In Virata's council chamber there were two
views expressed upon these matters. There were
some people, led by Krishna, who declared
that the Pandavas having served their sentence
and redeemed their pledge, should demand their
kingdom as a matter of right. But there were
others who felt that the Kauravas should not
be offended. They argued that as the Pandavas
had been foolish enough to stake their kingdom

in a game and lose it, they had forfeited their right to it. All they could do was to beg for kindness from Duryodhana and request a gift of land from him. The chief spokesman of this view was Krishna's brother, Balarama.

Drupada, swarthy-faced, proud and revengeful, was all for action.

In the end, Krishna, supported by the Pandavas and several other princes, suggested that they should try all means to avoid war. "Let us try every means to persuade the Kauravas," he said; "let us leave no stone unturned in the cause of peace; for the ways of peace are the best, and war is never an answer to a problem."

There were murmurs of approval from one section of the assembly, but Krishna had not finished. He went on: "The ways of peace are indeed the best. Yet there are times when men must choose war. For war is to be preferred to a cowardly peace bought at the price of men's honour." At this Drupada and his friends applauded.

"It is just what I say!" exclaimed Drupada. "War cannot be avoided. Do we not know the Kauravas and their crafty ways? We will have to wrest our rights from them by force, by war!"

Krishna however spoke firmly in favour of negotiations. "Seek the ways of peace," he advised them, "for war is a dreadful thing in which millions of lives would be sacrified. It is in our hands to try to prevent it."

Krishna's words raised a murmur of satisfaction among the assembled people. There was so much wisdom in them that even the proud and warlike Drupada had to agree reluctantly with what he said. On this note of peace the conference ended.

Only Draupadi listening intently, felt anger rise up in her like the fires of hell.

"Peace!" she cried out, turning on them with the fury of a tigress. "How can there be peace after the dishonour we have suffered?" Her voice broke and tears streamed down her face as she fell at Krishna's feet. "How can I forget their shameful treatment of me in their assembly? Can you not see that now is the time to avenge all the insults I suffered? O, how can you talk of peace?"

Krishna drew her aside and spoke to her words of comfort.

"Do not despair," he told her. "It is our duty to seek all ways of settling our demands peacefully. But mark my words—Duryodhana will reject every offer. In his pride and foolishness he will choose war instead of peace and in so doing he will bring about his own destruction."

"So be it!" uttered Draupadi fervently.

CHAPTER XXVII

ENVOYS AND MISSIONS

 URING the days that followed, the Pandavas and the Kauravas sent envoys to each other and exchanged messages in the hope of securing fair and honourable terms and of avoiding a fratricidal conflict. The first to go on behalf of the Pandavas was a trusted officer from Drupada's court. He came before Dhritarashtra and the Kauravas and, in the arrogant tone that Drupada had wished him to use, delivered his master's message faithfully. He reminded the Kauravas of the grievous wrongs they had done their cousins. In Drupada's name he demanded from them the kingdom Duryodhana had wrested from them by cunning and trickery. In no uncertain terms he warned them that if peaceful means failed to secure the Pandavas their rights, they would resort to war.

"Make no mistake about it!" he thundered. "The Pandavas are not afraid. They are fully armed and strenghthened by many alliances!"

Duryodhana's anger rose as he heard the envoy. But before he could answer, Bhishma spoke to him, pointing out the error of holding on to what did not rightly belong to him and warning him of the disaster that would overtake him if he did not act rightly. "Justice is justice," he said, "in however offensive a guise it may present itself."

Duryodhana turned on the old man, his face crimson with fury. "You love the Pandavas too much!" he accused him. "That is why you speak in this way!"

Karna sided with Duryodhana. Walking over to where he stood, Karna added his voice to that of his friend. "The Pandavas lost their inheritance by their own foolishness!" he said hotly. "How can they come now demanding it back! If they are prepared for war, why, so are we! Do they think we fear them?" He looked around with his usual swagger.

Bhishma, however, was not impressed by Karna's fine words and show of strength.

Dhritarashtra held up his hand. "I will send an envoy to Yudhishthira," he quavered. "Let us persuade the Pandavas to accept Duryodhana's decision and give up their claim to their inheritance. In this way we may avoid a war." Bhishma answered nothing, for he recognized Dhritarashtra's suggestion as an unworthy one. The foolish king was trying all kinds of dubious ways to avoid a conflict instead of facing the truth and doing the right thing.

Dhritarashtra's suggestion did not please Karna any more than it did Bhishma for Karna felt that it was cowardly. "Why should we be afraid of war?" Karna thought. "What is a Kshatriya worth if he will not face death and destruction with a smile?" But he too remained silent, for it was the king who had spoken. Dhritarashtra begged Sanjaya to go as his messenger to the Pandavas and persuade them to give in to Duryodhana. He was to speak to them in a mild and flattering tone, to appeal to their feelings of love for the family and respect for himself, and somehow prevent war.

Sanjaya came to Upalavya, the Matsyan city where the Pandavas had camped, and spoke to Yudhishthira as he had been asked to do.

"What is material wealth before the danger of death, Yudhishthira?" he said. "It is in your hands to avert a terrible war. Duryodhana will not listen to reason, but you are wise and good and thoughtful. Withdraw your claim to your inheritance and you will avert a great disaster."

Listening to these words, Yudhishthira felt confused and troubled, as Dhritarashtra had meant him to be. Yudhishthira was a man of peace, and now Dhritarashtra was requesting him to surrender his rights and those of his brothers for the sake of that very peace which he so passionately loved. He was persuading him to yield to wrong-doing, in the name of brotherly love and respect for elders; to give up his lawful inheritance and that of his brothers in order that Duryodhana might keep his unlawful gains.

Yudhishthira thought deeply and for long. Though he yearned for peace, he knew that if he chose Dhritarashtra's way he would be running away from his duty.

When he spoke at last, his voice was grave and earnest. "How can I do what you ask, Sanjaya?" he asked. "We wish our cousins well, for we belong to the same clan. We beg no more from them than that half of the kingdom which is our lawful inheritance." His voice shook with emotion and with sincerity. For a while he paused, unable to speak for the depth of his feeling. Then he stood up before Sanjaya and continued: "No more than our inheritance— but if Duryodhana will not agree even to this,

247

then let him give us only five villages—one for each of us as a token of his goodwill. Let him not deny us even a place to rest our limbs! Surely we cannot ask less than that."

Sanjaya went back to Hastinapura, bringing Yudhishthira's message to the Kaurava court. "They ask for just five villages!" he pleaded. "Their cause is just and they are strong."

'Strong!" Duryodhana laughed mockingly. "Is it their strength that makes them give up their claim to the kingdom and beg for five villages?"

Dhritarashtra tried to plead with his son. "They ask for so little, my child," he said, "give them five villages and they will be content."

Duryodhana lost his temper. "The Pandavas will have nothing," he shouted. "Not even the space of land that can be occupied by the point of a needle."

For one second a hushed silence fell on the hall. Then the voice of the elders rang out, warning Duryodhana. "Consider what you are doing!" they said. "You must be mad. Surely the time of your destruction must be near, for you seem to be intent on rushing to your death!"

But Duryodhana would listen to no advice.

It seemed indeed as if he had lost his reason and was rushing headlong towards his ruin!

Now when it seemed that all hope of a peaceful settlement was lost, Krishna himslf decided to go to Hastinapura and speak to the Kauravas. The Pandavas—even the lion-hearted Arjuna and Bhima—agreed that peace was to be preferred to war. Only Draupadi, remembering the great wrongs that had been done to her, cried shame upon her husbands for their hesitation in marching upon the men who had dishonoured her. "If my husbands are afraid," she taunted them, "let them say so, and I will go to my father Drupada and my brother Dhrishtadyumna. They and my five brave sons will come to my aid."

The Pandavas pitied her, for they understood how she felt. But they were wise and knew the dreadful destruction that war would bring. They were not cowards, but they did not wish to bring about such a great disaster. They sat silent, with bowed heads, unable to answer. But Krishna, who could see into all hearts and understand all things, drew her gently aside and begged her to take heart.

"There will be no peace, O Draupadi!" he assured her, as he climbed into his chariot. "The

Kauravas are drunk with power and will reject all our offers of peace!" Hearing his words, Draupadi felt happier. Krishna rode away while the Pandavas looked in the direction of the receding chariot with grave, anxious faces and prayerful hearts.

Krishna came before the assembly of the Kauravas where the members of the great Kuru clan sat waiting, and was led to the place of honour. From where he sat upon a beautiful throne, encrusted with jewels and precious stones, Krishna spoke to the Kauravas. In moving and eloquent language Krishna recounted how time and again the Kauravas had wronged and persecuted their cousins. He spoke of the game of dice, and of the humiliation of Draupadi and of how, true to their word, the Pandavas had lived in exile for thirteen gruelling years.

"These thirteen years have gone by," Krishna reminded the Kauravas. "The Pandavas have returned and now they claim the kingdom that was theirs! The world looks to you for justice."

As Krishna spoke, Duryodhana looked around him, and noticed how all who sat there listened to him with respect. He bit his lip fiercely. "How can the Pandavas claim what once they lost, O Krishna?" he demanded angrily. "Go back and tell them that they will get nothing from us!"

Once again the elders tried to persuade Duryodhana to see the error of his ways, and do right. Gandhari, his mother, came into the assembly hall and implored him to be reasonable, but Duryodhana, headstrong and proud paid no heed to her entreaties.

Krishna tried again. "Duryodhana!" said Krishna. "if you will not return to the Pandavas their kingdom, let them have at least five hundred villages!"

"No!" Duryodhana cried out, his voice bitter with hatred. "The Pandavas will have nothing!"

"Let them have fifty then!" Krishna pleaded. "It is not too much to ask, for the Pandavas are kings and sons of kings. Give them fifty villages, Duryodhana and they will be satisfied."

"No!" cried Duryodhana again. "No! No! No!" In the great hall the atmosphere was tense as a drawn bowstring, and in the silence one could have heard a pin drop.

Krishna spoke again, begging Duryodhana to think well and act rightly for the sake of peace, but Duryodhana only glowered at him and did not answer.

Krishna paused for a while before he resumed his speech.

"Listen, O Duryodhana," he said finally, "if you will not let them have even fifty, then let them have five villages."

Duryodhana flung back angrily, "Why do you waste your time babbling in this manner, Krishna? Have I not said already that the Pandavas will get nothing? Not even as much territory as will cover the point of a needle! Go and tell the Pandavas that."

He turned on his heel and left the hall. With him went his friends, Karna, Shakuni and the evilminded Dushahsana.

Krishna turned to the elders of the court. "You are wise and good men. You have knowledge and foresight," he appealed to them. "Duryodhana's greed and selfishness will lead to certain destruction. War will mean the annihilation of the entire race. O respected ones, I plead for better understanding and judgement. If it is only Duryodhana who stands between the Kuru race and disaster, then you must sacrifice Duryodhana. For he is only one individual and an individual may be sacrificed

252

in the interests of the larger group. If you remove Duryodhana you may yet save the situation and avert a war."

At this point Duryodhana burst into the room. "A plot," he cried. It is a plot to kill me! Seize him. Dushahsana, seize Krishna!" A plot it was indeed. But not to kill Duryodhana; it was Krishna's life which was in danger. At Duryodhana's words, Dushahsana sprang upon Krishna to bind him with ropes while the elders sat aghast; for all knew that it was against the universal law to lay hands upon an emissary.

"Stop!" they cried out, their voices resounding in the hall. "Stop, Duryodhana! Stop, Dushahsana!"

At this terrible moment a miracle happened, for Krishna showed himself in that instant in his divine form. Suddenly it seemed to those gathered there that he was everywhere and in all things, even in their own minds and hearts; and that all things were in him—the universe itself with the earth and the heavens, and all creation. As for Duryodhana, wherever he turned he seemed to see Krishna, while Dushahsana saw Krishna in every one who sat there, even in Duryodhana himself. He felt his senses reel. "Where are you, O Krishna?" he roared. "I

253

will seize you and bind you and make you prisoner. Where are you? Where? Where?". But dazed with the vision of Krishna in his divine form he never found Krishna. He never seized him and never took him prisoner and in the end he gave up in despair.

"It is a ruse!" Duryodhana muttered. "A trick to frighten us. But we will not yield an inch of territory."

In the midst of all the clamour and confusion, Krishna left the hall in a cloud of smoke.

In the assembly hall, all was as it had been before the miracle had taken place. In their hearts men had caught for an instant a glimpse of God. And the next minute things became as they had been before; nothing seemed to have changed.

The miracle was forgotten, while fear and foreboding hung in the air like a living thing.

But Krishna had gone from the Kaurava court. His mission had failed. He climbed into his chariot and drove away.

CHAPTER XXVIII

KUNTI MEETS KARNA

HEN Kunti heard that Krishna's mission had failed, that only war would decide the quarrel between the Pandavas and Kauravas, she was full of anxiety.

"Is it for this, my sons," she thought sadly to herself, "is it for this that you suffered so bravely and for so long, that you may be killed at last upon the field of battle, and your inheritance wrested from you by deceit and force?" She knew that Bhishma and Drona would never wish to kill the Pandavas; they loved them too dearly for that. It was Karna whom Kunti feared—Karna, that proud, invincible knight whose steadfast loyalty to Duryodhana was matched only by his implacable hatred for the Pandavas. Remembering Karna, Kunti's heart quailed. "O Karna," she cried, "my son, Karna! what cruel fate is this that finds you and your brothers on opposite sides of the battle-field? What unhappy fate has made you the foremost enemy of the Pandavas?"

All night Kunti lay awake tormented by conflicting thoughts. When dawn came, she got out of bed and slipping out of the palace alone and unseen, walked to the river bank where she knew Karna came each morning to say his prayers. Standing near him, she waited patiently until he had finished. When he turned round at last and greeted her courteously, she gathered up her courage and spoke to him. In a voice husky with emotion she told him the story of his birth and of how she had cast him adrift in the river many years ago.

"You are not the son of Adiratha and Radha at all, O Karna," she said. "The blood that runs in your veins is as royal as mine!"

Karna cast down his eyes. He answered nothing, and Kunti went on. "It is the truth I tell you, O Karna: I am your mother."

Still Karna answered nothing. Unable to bear the silence any longer, Kunti cried out at last, begging him with clasped hands, to forgive her for the wrong she had done him. But Karna harboured no anger against her.

"What is there to forgive, O my mother?" he said in a low voice. "Fate rules all men and controls their actions. It has been your destiny that you should have borne me and cast me

Karna... answered nothing.

away; it has been mine that I should have been brought up by strangers and lived to see this day." He begged her not to ask for forgiveness and assured her gently that his heart held no resentment.

At Karna's words a great weight seemed to lift from Kunti's heart. She steeled herself to the effort and told him what was in her mind. "You are the eldest of the Pandavas," she said. "Surely you cannot fight against them, for you are bound to them by ties of blood."

Then speaking quickly and breathlessly she begged Karna to come and join his brothers.

"You are a royal prince," she reminded him, "and you must live like one. At the Kaurava court you are no more than a servant. However high you may rise in their favour, they will always be your masters. But if you join your brothers then you will rule and not serve. Your royal birth will be recognized, and as the eldest son you will be king. You will have wealth and power and all their inheritance. Come, Karna, come and take your rightful place among those who are your flesh and blood."

But Karna was not to be bought over in this manner. Kunti did not know the stuff of which he was made. He faced her boldly and spoke

quite simply. "How can you ask this of me?"
he said. "For many years, I have lived at the
Kaurava court and all that I have today, all
that I am today, I owe to the Kauravas and to
Duryodhana. Now, in the hour of their need
when they depend upon me to bring them
victory in the war, would you wish me to forsake my life-long friends and change sides?
Would this be conduct befitting a prince, a
Kshatriya, an honourable man?"

As he went on, his voice was like a whip
lashing her. "If, tempted by your offer of crown
and wealth, I acted in this low and cowardly
manner, how could I show my face to the
world? Do you not see, O Kunti, that by acting
as you advise me to do I would bring ruin and
not glory upon myself? Do you not see that I
would know no peace? And if a man is not at
peace with himself, then what would he gain
even if he had all the wealth of the world?"

Karna spoke boldly, and as she heard him
Kunti felt her heart stir with pride. She knew
that here before her stood a true Kshatriya, a
prince among men, one who could never be
bribed or bought. She was torn between admiration for him and anxiety for the Pandavas.
And yet she would not give up. She tried another

way. This time she appealed to his duty as a son.

"By the laws of Dharma," she persisted, "children owe their parents love and respect and obedience. Surely you, a man of law, will not disregard your mother's plea?"

At these words a look of deep bitterness came over Karna's handsome face. There was a long silence before he could bring himself to say anything. At last in a low voice he spoke to her, reminding her of the wrong she had done him.

"What duty do I owe you, O my mother?" he said. "Forsaken in infancy, I was left to die by you who gave me birth! Have you done a mother's duty by me? Have you given me a mother's love? Having denied me this, what claim have you now upon me? I grew up among strangers, and these many years your son mattered nothing to you. Do you not see that my real parents are Adiratha and Radha? How can I forsake them who have loved me and cared for me all these years?"

Kunti covered her face with her hands, and the scalding tears flowed down her cheeks. She could not bear to hear his words, but he went on relentlessly.

"All these years you have had no thought for

me. But now that the lives of your other sons
are in danger you come to me. Even at this
moment it is for them that you plead!"

Karna did not speak in anger, only in sorrow.
Hard though it was to hear his reproaches,
Kunti knew that he spoke the truth. She had
never given him a mother's love. How then could
she claim from him a son's duty? Weeping
softly, Kunti turned to go.

Karna looked at her and suddenly he felt
his heart stir with pity. She seemed so weak, so
helpless. She had begged a favour from him,
and he who had never refused anyone anything
had turned her, his mother, away. "Wait!" he
said at last, "Wait, O my mother!" Kunti
waited, trembling to think that he would reproach her again. But when he spoke this time
his voice was quiet and gentle.

"I cannot join the Pandavas," Karna said.
"But this I will promise you, my mother, since
you come to me begging for their lives: I shall
spare the lives of four of the five Pandavas—
Yudhishthira, Bhima, Nakula and Sahadeva:
these four, I shall not kill. But I cannot promise
more than this. I cannot promise you Arjuna's
life. Arjuna I shall fight and try with all my
strength and power to kill. Either Arjuna or

I must die, for there is no room on this earth for both of us. And so, O my mother, when one of us is gone, you will still have five sons, for one of us will live!"

Tears flowed down Kunti's wrinkled face. "How noble you are, O Karna!" she whispered. "How can I ask more than this? May the Gods bless you!"

Karna saluted her, prostrating himself before her, and she touched his head in blessing. Then before he could rise, she turned and walked swiftly back to the palace.

CHAPTER XXIX

PREPARATIONS FOR WAR

O THE Pandavas waiting anxiously at Upalavya Krishna brought the terrible news from Hastinapura that all his efforts to secure an honourable peace had failed and that Duryodhana was adamant. All paths were closed to them now save that of war.

Listening to him, the Pandavas grew grave and heavy-hearted, but Draupadi gave a cry of joy, "Revenge!" she cried out. "Oh, sweet, sweet revenge that now will be ours. Now our wrongs will be avenged! Now Dushahsana's blood will flow and soak the earth! Now the wicked Duryodhana's life will end at the hands of Bhima! Now the Kauravas who brought shame and sorrow on me will be destroyed, root and branch!"

But Yudhishthira did not share her feelings. The news that Krishna brought left him unhappy and disturbed. For a long time he turned it over in his mind, but he could see nothing he could do at this stage. The die was cast; there was no turning back. Krishna left the Pandavas and returned to his capital, Dwaraka.

Now both parties began to prepare for war. They sent their emissaries to the courts of other rulers of the day with a view to gaining support and military help.

The kings of the various realms listened attentively to their messages. For many of them it was not easy to decide. Two branches of the same family were going to fight a war. To many kings both the Pandavas and the Kauravas were related by the same ties of blood. Many people who sympathised with the Pandavas were afraid of the military power of the Kauravas. There were others who felt that the Pandavas had no right to a throne which they had gambled away through their own foolishness.

Balarama and Krishna were related both to the Kauravas and to the Pandavas. Balarama felt he could not join either side without doing injustice to his relatives on the other. He declared himself neutral, and Yudhishthira seeing the truth of his reasoning did not try to persuade him against his will. But there was Krishna to be reckoned with. The Yadava armies were large and well-trained. Duryodhana was anxious to secure them. He came personally to Dwaraka to meet Krishna and gain his support.

Now it happened that, by a curious coincidence, Arjuna also arrived on the same day at Krishna's palace with the same purpose in mind. The guards, knowing them to be relatives of the prince, showed them both into the inner rooms. As they entered they saw Krishna lying asleep on his silken couch. And so they must needs wait until he awoke. The story goes that they took their seats—Duryodhana, haughtily choosing the golden chair that stood at the head of the bed, Arjuna happy to sit on a low stool at the sleeping Krishna's feet. Thus they waited in silence, each thinking in his heart his own thoughts unknown to the other. Arjuna's mind dwelt on Krishna,—on Krishna's goodness and wisdom and power. But Duryodhana's mind was full of bitterness and anger against his cousins, and full too of his own importance and wealth and might. Presently Krishna awoke and sat up and in so doing his eyes fell first on Arjuna whom he greeted. And there was in his voice such warmth and pleasure that Duryodhana sitting high on his golden chair, felt a stab of anger and envy. He coughed gently to attract attention and Krishna turned round and saw him.

"What good fortune is mine!" exclaimed Krishna. "What good fortune to have two of my dearest relatives and friends visit me to-gether!" And he held out his arms in welcome and drew them both to him. Then he placed them on either side of him on his couch and did them equal honour. With his own hands he brought them water to wash their feet; and after they had washed he served them food and drink and he spoke to them and enquired after their own welfare and health and the welfare and health of their families. Then after these formalities were completed, he asked them very gently the reason for their visit.

"I come to seek your help in the war, cousin Krishna," Duryodhana said to him speaking first. "You will do well to come on our side for we are strong: our numbers are large and our victory is certain." Krishna turned to Arjuna, "And you, Arjuna, what brings you here?" Arjuna answered: "I came also for the same reason, dear cousin—to beg for your help, for without it we are nothing and less than nothing." His voice was low and humble.

Krishna's brow knitted in mock surprise and his merry eyes twinkled. "This is awkward, my cousins," he laughed, "that both of you should

come at the same time for the same thing."
Then growing serious he regarded them thought-
fully for a minute, looking from one to the
other, his handsome face cupped in his hands.
Finally he stood up and spoke: "You know
that I and my forces are both at your disposal,"
he said. "There is nothing I would not spare for
either of you, for you are both related to me
by close ties of blood. But I would like to be
completely just and fair, and give my help to
both. Let Krishna never be accused of having
helped one brother against the other. Therefore, I will leave the choice to you. The choice
shall be between my forces and me. You may
have either my forces or me but you cannot
have both. He who chooses me to be on his
side may have me, but my armies will fight
then for the other. I alone will be on his side,
and I will neither bear arms nor take part in
the fighting. It is for you to choose!"

Duryodhana was about to choose but Krishna
held him back:

"You were both here at the same time," he
said. "But I saw Arjuna first. So let it be Arjuna
who chooses first." Duryodhana protested violently, that it was a trick to hoodwink him,
but Krishna silenced him saying that in all

games there was always a small element of
luck. Duryodhana scowled darkly. He had
never trusted Krishna. Now he was sure that
Krishna was going to double-cross him. But
all the while that Krishna was speaking Arjuna
had been gazing steadfastly into his face, his
heart full reverence and love. He lost no time
in making his choice, for he had no doubts.
He chose Krishna. "If you be on our side, what
more can we want, Lord?" he said deeply
moved. Krishna turned to Duryodhana. A few
minutes ago that prince had been protesting
bitterly. But now he stood looking as if he could
not believe his ears. His good luck seemed too
good to be true. No man —Duryodhana felt,—
no man in his senses could have thrown away
such a chance as Arjuna had done! Well, that
was lucky for him! And Arjuna had only himself to blame! He said briskly, to indicate that
the matter was ended and there was no more
to be said: "Your armies for me then, Krishna.
It is settled: Arjuna himself has settled it so."
For he was afraid Arjuna might change his
mind. Arjuna, however, seemed content with
the arrangement. Duryodhana looked at him
contemptuously. "This Arjuna is a fool," Duryodhana thought. "For who but an utter fool,

would make such a choice and throw away the last chance of victory?" He gave a self-satisfied smirk and congratulated himself upon having won the victory even before the war had started.

He had good reason to be confident. There were others whose support he was sure of. The terrible Jayadratha or Saindhava, giant among men, king of the Sindhu and husband of his sister, was on his side. So were Susharama, king of the Trigartas, and his sons, all mighty warriors of the time. Then there was Shalya,—king of Madra Desha and maternal uncle of Nakula and Sahadeva. The wily Duryodhana had tricked and bribed Shalya into promising to fight on the Kaurava side against his nephews. Duryodhana smiled gleefully remembering how he had tricked the unsuspecting Shalya into the situation.

Shalya, concerned about his nephews, had set out from his kingdom on the journey to Upalavya. Now Duryodhana hearing this had hastened to work out the cunning scheme he had devised. All along the road that he knew Shalya was travelling, he had had wells dug for thirsting travellers and water troughs constructed for animals. He had built rest-houses and inns where travellers could sleep and eat and refresh themselves. Here they could get fresh horses if their own were tired. Slaves and servants waited upon Shalya and his retinue at these resting places and they were fed upon the tastiest foods and regaled with the choicest of wines. Musicians and dancers and acrobats performed for the travellers and entertained them in the evenings. Shalya's journey which would otherwise have been a long and arduous one became so pleasant that he was enthralled. "Why, Yudhishthira has been kindness itself!" Shalya exlaimed, certain that no one but Yudhishthira could have been so generous or provided so many conforts—"How can I withhold my help from one who has done so much for me, and whose hospitality I have so freely accepted?"

And when people asked him whom he would support in the war, he answered laughing: "Naturally that prince who has been my kind host." Shalya had a rude shock when he heard that that kind host had been Duryodhana and not Yudhishthira as he had fondly imagined! Duryodhana met him at one stage of the journey and enlightened Shalya. "If you are a man of your word," the Kaurava reminded him, "then you must fight on our side and give us your support!" Shalya was completely taken aback. He had never dreamed things would take such a turn. Nakula and Sahadeva were his sister's sons and he loved them dearly. He had the greatest respect for Yudhishthira, and Arjuna had always been a good friend of his. Duryodhana's trick made him look foolish. Shalya felt he had been cheated, but he could not deny that Duryodhana now had a hold on him. Having accepted Duryodhana's hospitality he could not fight against him. Reluctantly Shalya agreed to fight on the Kaurava side. But he remained uneasy and unhappy. He loved the Pandavas too well to want their defeat and death. Little did Duryodhana realize that this unwilling ally he had bought over would not prove a steadfast, faithful friend. To him it seemed that with the allies he had collected and the armies he had built up, victory was as good as won. Duryodhana hurried away from Dwaraka and returned to Hastinapura in high spirits.

Arjuna took leave of Krishna. They would meet again shortly, for Krishna had promised to follow him to Upalavya as soon as he could. Arjuna arriving at the Pandava camp, found his brother and their allies busy with preparations for the war. He approached Yudhishthira and related to him the happenings at Dwaraka. When he told Yudhishthira about the choice he had made the latter was full of joy. He embraced his brother warmly and told him he had chosen wisely and well. "With Krishna on our side, armed or unarmed, we have nothing to fear," he said fervently. Then he remembered Shalya and his face grew worried. He decided to speak to Krishna about it when he came.

"Shalya could never have gone over willingly to the Kauravas," said Krishna when he heard. "There must have been some misunderstanding." So indeed there was as he found out when he spoke to Shalya. He sent to Shalya's camp to speak to him. He found too that Shalya had no real sympathy for Duryodhana. He was willing even at this stage to render assistance to the Pandavas if he could do so without Duryodhana's knowing. Krishna said to him "O Shalya, there is much that you can do. You know that there is no charioteer like you in the world. It is certain that Karna will choose you to be his chariot driver. You will drive him over the battle-field and be with him when he faces Arjuna, and thus you will hold Arjuna's life in your hands. Karna will depend on you to render him assistance in the battle between him and Arjuna. He will depend on you to steer his chariot skilfully and bring him to victory. If you love Arjuna, O Shalya, you will know what to do."

Shalya who was listening carefully, nodded. "I know what I must do, O Krishna," he said. "I have never loved the arrogant Karna. He will get his deserts for I am and always shall be Arjuna's friend."

Krishna thanked him warmly and returned to Upalavya. In the Pandava camp he found Yudhishthira going about his duties with energy and determination. His brothers and his allies all looked to him to lead them to victory. Yudhishthira appointed seven able generals to command the seven divisions of their army. Drupada, Dhrishtadyumna, Shikhandin, Virata, Satyaki, Chekidhana and Bhima. Of these Dhrishtadyumna was chosen as Supreme Commander of the entire army. Yudhishthira would have liked Krishna to have taken this position, but Krishna declined, smiling. "I have promised Duryodhana that I will not take up arms or fight," he said. "If I must take part in the war, let me be Arjuna's charioteer."

The others looked at him in amazement.

"The great prince of Dwaraka a charioteer?" they thought to themselves. But they said nothing, for they trusted Krishna completely.

Krishna was Arjuna's charioteer during the eighteen days that the great war of Kurukshetra was fought.

Now on the eve of Kurukshetra a hot quarrel had flared up in the camp of the Kauravas, and there was angry disagreement among their warriors. Bhishma, the veteran hero of many wars and supreme commander of the Kaurava forces, had been given the task of appointing the commanding officers. It was expected that Karna would be appointed to a very high rank. But Bhishma had never approved of Karna's arrogance and high-handed manner. Karna for his part disliked Bhishma and doubted his loyalty to the Kaurava cause. When the time came for choosing the officers, Bhishma spoke his mind frankly to Duryodhana and showed his open disapproval of Karna. Cut to the quick, Karna answered back sharply—and a wordy war followed between them. Incensed by Bhishma's words, Karna declared hotly that he would not take up arms or fight as long as Bhishma was commander. Here was a pretty pass! Duryodhana was vexed and grieved. He

tried to persuade Karna to take a more reasonable attitude. But Karna's pride would not
allow him to swallow what he considered an
insult. In the end Duryodhana had to agree to
Karna's staying out of the war

CHAPTER XXX

KURUKSHETRA AND AFTER

I

THE WAR BEGINS

HE day of the battle dawned bright and clear; in the sunshine the banners of the kings and chieftains who took part in the great Kurukshetra war fluttered like many-coloured birds. The air resounded with the fearful sounds that precede a great battle: the echoing and re-echoing of conch shells, the roll of war drums, the neighing and whinnying of horses and the dreadful trumpeting of elephants.

In his chariot Arjuna sat silently gazing into the distance at the armies on the other side. He could make out the figures who stood in the front ranks: Bhishma, his great uncle, head of the Kuru clan; Drona and Kripa, his teachers; and his cousins, the hundred Kauravas. Looking at these people whom he had loved, who were his close relatives, bound to him by ties of blood, Arjuna suddenly felt his brave heart fail him. His eyes filled with tears, his knees began to tremble, and the bow he held began to slip from his hand. How could he kill them and shed their blood? To what purpose? What would he gain by destroying those whom he loved and revered? What happiness would empire or kingship or power bring him if in the end these things were to be gained by the destruction of fellow human beings: relatives and friends and boyhood companions? Arjuna's heart faltered and tears rolled down his cheeks. Suddenly he threw away his arms and sat down, crying out: "O Krishna, I will not fight this war. I cannot bring myself to destroy those whom I love and honour. Let us surrender. Let the Kauravas take everything, so that there may be peace and goodwill."

It was a moment of crisis. A great battle was about to begin and all was in readiness for it. And just as the first shot was to be fired the foremost warrior of the day had suddenly lost courage. It seemed to him so senseless and futile to fight and kill and shed blood—all for the sake of a patch of land called a kingdom.

Krishna listened to Arjuna's words with compassion. He saw how the blood had drained from the hero's face leaving it pale and grey. He saw how he trembled and how his hair stood on end. Then Krishna spoke wise and gentle words to his friend upon that field of battle, cheering and encouraging him and giving him heart. For Krishna knew that it was too late now to withdraw from the conflict or to have second thoughts. The Pandavas had committed themselves, and now they must go through with the fight to the very end. He spoke to Arjuna of many things on that memorable day: of life and of death; of this world and the ones that are invisible; of the struggles and conflicts and sorrows of mankind; of the three paths by which men may reach God: for all may reach God, no matter who or what they were. There were endless roads that led to Him, but of them all, there were three that were best known—the path of meditation and yoga, the path of duty and the path of love. Each man, said Krishna, may choose his own path to God according to his nature. But for the Kshatriya, as for most people, the way to God lay in the path of duty. Men must work and in their work find God. Arjuna was a Kshatriya and his duty

was to fight for righteousness, whatever the consequences. The time for doubt was gone now,
said Krishna. Now was the time for action and
there must be no hesitation. Arjuna must act
fearlessly. And when he acted he must do so
without the desire or hope of reward or glory
or even success. Right action, said Krishna, was
that which was free from all desire—even the
desire for success.

Last of all Krishna spoke to Arjuna of the
limitless and one God that men seek. "I will
speak to you of My divine forms," he said,
"but only those which are the most important
for I am infinite. I am the beginning, the middle
and the end of everything. For I am birth and
the beginning of all things; I am death which
is the end. I am eternal, for I was never born;
neither will I ever die. I exist everywhere in
all things, and all things exist in Me. There is
nothing moving or unmoving that can exist
without Me!"

As Arjuna listened, strange emotions seized
him. It came to him like the dawning of light
upon darkness that here was no small mortal
who sat beside him, but God himself. Understanding this feebly, he began to long to see
God in all His glory, and spoke his desire to

Krishna. Then Krishna revealed himself to his friend. And Arjuna saw the heavenly vision and was struck with such amazement and fear, that his senses reeled and he trembled violently like a leaf in a storm. For the vision was limitless as the universe itself. All around him was the Divine Form, infinite and unending. Across the skies it blazed and over the earth, in all things— even in the smallest particle—a wondrous form such as he could not describe, for he was blinded by the light of countless Suns. There was neither beginning nor end and gazing upon it Arjuna felt breathless as if he was a speck of dust and less than that, drowning in a vast endless sea. Fear seized him and his voice cried out to Krishna for help. Then the Lord in His mercy returned to his human form. The vision ceased and all things became as they were. Nothing seemed to have changed. All was as it had been before everywhere except in Arjuna's heart. For of a sudden it seemed to Arjuna that the scales had fallen from his eyes, and he had seen with the eyes of wisdom. He joined his hands and worshipped Krishna in his heart. Then with new spirit surging through him he took up his arms again and went into battle.

So the war began. It continued for eighteen

days and everyday blood flowed in rivers drench-
ing the earth; and the dead and the dying lay
in mangled heaps upon the ground. At sunset
each day the truce was sounded, and the warriors
rested in their camps while the sentries kept
watch outside. During the war men showed
themselves in their true natures: all their strength
and their weaknesses came to light: many deeds
of valour and chivalry were done; but the weaker
side of their natures revealed itself too in moments
of crisis, and great and good men stooped often
to unworthy things like falsehood and treachery
and forgot the noble lessons of Kshatriya conduct—of human conduct.

On the first day, with Dushahsana leading
the Kauravas, and Bhima the Pandavas, the
armies came to grips, and after many hours of
fearful fighting, a terrible duel took place between Arjuna's son, Abhimanyu, and Bhishma,
the grandsire of the clan. For Bhishma pierced
the Pandava army formation that first day,
bringing with him death and such terror that
no one could withstand him. Swift and sure
flew his deadly arrows, and men fell before them
like insects in a fire. Panic spread among the
Pandava forces as they fought desperately to
hold their ground. But Bhishma's advance could

not be checked, and it seemed that the Pandavas would be routed completely on the very first day. Then the young Abhimanyu came riding in his chariot to meet the fiery old warrior in combat. He fought with astonishing skill and courage. Here was one who did not know what fear was, and danger only made him the more eager to go out and meet it. Men looked at the boy in wonder, for he seemed to be everywhere, at all times, fighting in turn with bow and mace and sword with such dexterity that it took the combined efforts of Bhishma, Shalya, Kripa and Kirtivarman to beat him back. Still he fought on, one youth scarcely out of his boyhood, amongst these fierce and hardened warriors, eager-eyed and undaunted, until the Pandavas, fearing for his safety, sent to his help Virata and his sons Sweta and Uttara Kumar. Then the enemy turned their attack on these and in the fierce fight that followed the noble sons of Virata were slain. Bhishma followed up the victory by leading an attack on the Pandava army and routing it completely.

On the second day, however, the Pandavas recovered their strength because of the brave leadership and the determination of Arjuna, Dhrishtadyumna and Bhima. On this second day

Arjuna met the unconquerable Bhishma in a battle; but so well matched were they that neither could win or lose. Besides, though he had steeled himself to destroy Bhishma, at the sight of that brave veteran, his great-uncle whom he loved and venerated, the head of his family who had been more than a father to him, Arjuna could not bring himself to put forth his best effort. The battle thus ended in a draw. But that same day on another front the Pandavas fighting under Dhrishtadyumna and Bhima won a great victory.

II

BHISHMA'S FALL

Day after day the warriors fought. Sometimes it seemed that one side won, and sometimes the other. Mighty deeds were done on both sides. But it was Bhishma who, time and again, carried the day; there was no one like him, for he had had many years of experience and was unconquerable. Wherever Bhishma went, he brought death and terror and destruction, and made the enemy fly as from a wild fire. It was all the Pandavas could do to keep up their courage before his onslaughts, for surely they would have been defeated and totally destroyed, if Arjuna's deeds of valour had not repeatedly saved the day and allowed them breathing space. No less remarkable were the deeds of Arjuna's valiant son, Abhimanyu. Time and again this gallant lad was put to the test; time and again he emerged victorious. His courage never once failed him, and undaunted he led many attacks upon the enemy. Arjuna's heart swelled with pride as he saw how, when surrounded upon all sides by fierce Kaurava warriors, Abhimanyu fought back like a young lion, single-handed, never once turning back, never despairing. Bhima was there too, fighting with great courage, cutting down one after another the brothers of Duryodhana, for he had sworn to destroy them. And beside Bhima stood his son, Ghatot-kacha, whose mother was Hidimba. But even their combined efforts were of no avail against the mighty Bhishma, whose attacks were like those of the God of Death himself.

Again and again Krishna spoke to Arjuna, charging him to conquer Bhishma, for with Bhishma alive Krishna knew that victory would never be won. But Arjuna, in spite of all his

resolutions, shrank from the terrible deed. He
loved Bhishma too deeply. Every day the battles
raged, and great numbers of men fell upon the
battle-field; the armies moved up and down
and back and forth but Arjuna's heart cried
out against the slaying of Bhishma, and he
could not bring himself to do it. On the ninth
day of the war Bhishma was still alive and
strong as ever, and Krishna seeing how he
pushed back the Pandavas with his might, lost
his patience with Arjuna for the half-hearted
manner in which he fought. Jumping from the
chariot he took his discus in his hand, crying
out that if Arjuna would not slay Bhishma then
he would do the deed himself. But Arjuna held
him back greatly distressed, for he did not wish
Krishna to go back on the word he had given
Duryodhana that he would not bear arms or
fight in the war. He did not wish Krishna to be
false. "Tomorrow I will kill Bhishma " Arjuna
promised. "O Krishna, wait until tomorrow,"
and Krishna was pleased.

Arjuna kept his word. On the tenth day he
brought Bhishma down, but only by adopting
means that were blatantly unfair. For Arjuna,
even Arjuna, as Krishna reminded him, was
no match against the mighty son of Ganga.

285

Man to man, if Bhishma fought back, Arjuna stood no chance against him, so strong was his arm, so deadly his aim. It was therefore for them to see that Arjuna did not confront Bhishma in a straight encounter. It was only thus he could be rendered powerless.

"Bhishma scrupulously obeys the laws of the Kshatriya code," Krishna reminded Arjuna. "Come what may, he will not raise his hand against a woman or one born as a woman. Therefore bring Shikhandin, and place him before you in your war chariot; then from behind Shikhandin take aim and shoot your darts. Bhishma will never fight Shikhandin, for all the world knows that he was born as a woman!"

Arjuna heard these words with a grieving heart. Where was this dreadful war leading them? Into what morass of wrong doing and unrighteousness? Yet now that they were in the war, victory must be won. Arjuna steeled his heart and made his decision. Bhishma would die.

On the tenth day men saw Arjuna's shining chariot moving swiftly through the army formations. Shikhandin of Panchala stood in it where Arjuna should have stood, his bow poised for action. Arjuna himself crouched behind him, hidden from view. From this vantage point Arjuna shot his arrows. So fast did they fly and so sure was their aim that men knew at once that these were not the arrows of the prince of Panchala, but of one far mightier and more skilled than he could ever be.

From his own chariot Bhishma looked up, and then he smiled, for he understood everything. Now was the hour of his fall. He had been true all his life, but he was to be brought down by untruth! Bhishma did not mind. Death he knew must come to all men, and he who had lived a life of honour and goodness did not flinch from it.

He saw Shikhandin and remembered the vow that Amba had taken long years ago to destroy him—Amba whom he had unintentionally wronged had been born for this and blessed by Shiva, the God of the destruction. Bhishma laid down his arms. He would never fight one who had been born a woman. Even in the face of death, Bhishma scorned to do something which he considered ignoble and unchivalrous. So he stood waiting for his death while the arrows came swift and thick and struck him on every side; they struck at his shield and shattered it. They struck him through his armour and pierced his flesh in so many places that there was not a needle point of space left anywhere upon his body. But he would neither strike back nor turn and run. He stood there like a gallant old lion in his strength, until there came from the bow of Arjuna one deadly arrow with the speed of lightning and pierced his heroic heart.

Bhishma laughed when he saw it, for he knew it was Arjuna's arrow, and the knowledge pleased him as he fell mortally wounded.

A loud cry went up from the people who saw him fall. The news spread like wild fire; the people, stunned by it, dropped their weapons and the fighting ceased. They came running to where he lay, and the two parties called a truce as they gathered around him, while a sudden hush fell upon the field of battle. Then they all came forward to do him homage, for they knew his greatness and recognized him for a hero such as the world had never seen. Friend and foe alike came and honoured him as a soldier, strong of arm and stout of heart; honest and true to his beliefs; open and outspoken, hating everything that was mean and ignoble, and of a courage unflinching and unfaltering in the hour of danger. When they came to his side

...for he knew it was Arjuna's arrow...as he fell
mortally wounded.

they saw how his body did not touch the ground, but was held up on the arrows that had pierced it.

"Look!" they whispered, "The warrior lies upon a bed of arrows. What bed could be more fitting for such a soldier as he was?"

But he was tormented by pain. His head hung down as he lay gasping for breath. "A support for my head," he gasped. But when they brought him cushions and pillows he smiled gently and whispered, "These are not the pillows that I would use." He turned his eyes upon Arjuna, who nodded, for he alone, of all of them there, understood the old warrior's meaning.

Then Arjuna took three arrows from his quiver and shot them one after another in quick succession so that they struck the earth where Bhishma's head hung; and the warriors who had gathered there lifted it up and placed it upon the arrows to give it support. Then Bhishma smiled and was happy, for now there was no part of him that had not been touched by the enemy's arrows.

Now when all the warriors had paid their respects, Karna came to Bhishma's side. During Bhishma's life Karna had hated him bitterly. The two men, both so brave and honourable, had never seen eye to eye on any subject. Karna had stayed out of the fight because Bhishma had been chosen commander. He had always doubted Bhishma's loyalty to the Kaurava cause; but now, as Bhishma lay upon the battle-field pierced by Arjuna's arrows, Karna knew that Bhishma had been true. Kneeling now at Bhishma's side, he asked for forgiveness which Bhishma readily and ungrudgingly gave. Duryodhana came too and Bhishma, fixing his dying gaze upon him, begged him again to make peace with his cousins even at this stage. Peace was infinitely better than war, Bhishma told him, and the Pandava cause was just. But Duryodhana hardened his heart against the old warrior's advice:

"That I cannot do!" he said, "I will fight till the bitter end." Bhishma grieved sorely for the misguided prince.

Presently his mouth and lips grew parched with thirst and he gasped for water. But when they brought it to him in gold and silver vessels he would not take it. He fixed his eyes on Arjuna, who alone understood his meaning. Arjuna shot an arrow into the earth, causing a spring of cool, clear water to bubble out and reach the dying warrior's lips. Then he drank this sweet water and it refreshed him as he lay there. And yet, it was not time for him to go.

"The sun is in the southern regions of the earth," he whispered to them. "Until he begins his northward journey death must keep away from me."

For many years ago when Bhishma was young, his father had blessed him and declared that death itself would not conquer him unless he wished it to do so.

"I will lie here upon the field of battle," Bhishma said, "until the sun makes his return journey and lights up the northern part of the world."

Then one by one at his bidding the men left him, and went to their places to continue the fight. But Bhishma lay upon his bed of arrows while the days passed. Around him the war waged with the wild cries of frenzied men and the throb of drums, the twanging of bowstrings, the trumpeting of elephants and the neighing of horses. The arrows whizzed over his head and around him like golden rain, but Bhishma's mind remained clear and unclouded to the end and his heart was at peace.

III

ABHIMANYU

On Bhishma's fall Karna was chosen by Duryodhana to be commander-in-chief of the Kaurava army. But Karna stepped aside and yielded place to Drona, who was older and more experienced.

On the eleventh day of the war Duryodhana, planning the operations, commanded Drona to bend his efforts to the capture of Yudhishthira. If Yudhishthira was captured alive, Duryodhana reasoned secretly to himself, he could be enticed into yet another game of dice and defeated. Such a defeat would be so much easier to accomplish than a defeat upon the battle-field.

Drona, reluctant at heart, had nevertheless to agree. Duryodhana was his master, and obedience, he knew, was the first duty of a soldier.

So Drona went into battle, and swooping down upon the Pandava lines with fierce and determined thrusts, routed them, and made his way to the heart of the formation where he knew Yudhishthira would be. It was no mean or easy task for even so great a soldier as Drona, for Arjuna, alerted by what was happening and guessing Drona's objective, sprang to the defence of his brother and king. Arjuna was fighting now on two fronts; his attention was divided between the savage attacks of the sons of Susharma on one side, some distance away, and those of Drona on the other. Susharma's sons, the Samsaptakas, were reckless in their daring. Seeing how the war had gone badly for their side, they had come together and sworn to go into the thickest of the fight and never retreat. Only death was to stop their advance; and in the event of the death of one brother another was to step into his place and go steadily on.

Never was such desperate courage seen. It seemed to Arjuna that they fought more like demons than human beings. It was all he could do to withstand their impetuous and determined onslaughts.

In the midst of this Arjuna received the news of Drona's thrust into the Pandava lines, and his attack on Yudhishthira's defences.

Seizing a moment's respite when the Samsaptakas had been thrown off their guard, and making hurried arrangements for checking their advance, Arjuna rushed to his brother's help.

Backwards and forwards went Arjuna on that eleventh day of the battle, his attention divided equally between the attacks of the Samsaptakas on the one hand, and of Drona on the other. On the twelfth day the position worsened, for on that day Drona broke through the Pandava army and would surely have captured Yudhishthira during Arjuna's absence had Bhima not rescued him at the very last moment.

The thirteenth day of the battle dawned. The fighting was growing more desperate and fearful, while no side could yet claim victory over the other and neither would give in. On the thirteenth day, however, Arjuna determined to bring the battle with the Samsaptakas to an end, for it had gone on too long and had sapped the energy of the Pandava army. For a while Drona's advance had been checked. Arjuna did not doubt that Yudhishthira would be safe. So he begged Krishna to drive his chariot to the scene of the Samsaptaka attack.

Now when Arjuna was gone, Yudhishthira found himself face to face with Drona. He noted how Drona had arranged his army in the shape of a wheel. For a while his attack had been repulsed, but Yudhishthira knew that Drona was waiting for the first opportunity to advance and take him prisoner. It seemed to Yudhishthira that the best way to prevent this would be to wrest the advantage from their hands by launching an offensive and attacking the enemy boldly. But the enemy who had pierced the Pandava phalanx had planted themselves in a tight ring and Yudhishthira knew that the manoeuvre was a complicated one, and few people knew how to break it up. Among the Pandavas there were only four who had any knowledge of it. They were Arjuna, Krishna, Pradyumna and Abhimanyu, Arjuna's young son. Arjuna, Krishna and Pradyumna were away. Yudhishthira therefore sent for Abhimanyu and spoke to him of his plan.

"Would you be willing to lead the attack on Drona's units?" he asked "You, my child, are the only one who has any knowledge of the wheel formation of the army."

The boy Abhimanyu gladly and eagerly accepted the leadership of the army, proud that so great a task had been entrusted to him. So eager was he indeed that he did not stop to think how he would make his way out of the enemy lines if he was surrounded and overpowered. High-spirited and reckless as he was, it did not occur to Abhimanyu in his youth to think of the need for any plans for a retreat. "I will go, my uncle," cried he, and Yudhishthira embraced him and blessed him.

Then Abhimanyu ordered his charioteer to make for the Kaurava army, and he stood up in it as it sped away, eager-eyed and smiling like a young God. Yudhishthira watched him go and suddenly his heart misgave him. Had he done right? What if Abhimanyu failed? He was little more than a child, and he had sent this raw youth out into the heart of the battle.

But Abhimanyu felt no doubts. His heart soared with hope, for he did not know what fear was. Yudhishthira had promised to send others after him to help him. Abhimanyu did not doubt that they would come. But the attack, he knew, had to be made by one individual. He had to break his way through and only then could the others in his unit follow.

Abhimanyu rushed at the enemy lines. So great was the fury of his attack that the rings broke before him, and he pierced them one after another. The enemy was taken completely by surprise. Abhimanyu's chariot entered the enemy formation. The boy gave a cry of triumph. He had achieved what few had been able to do. But, now came the tragedy, for as soon as he entered, the Kaurava soldiers, recovering from their initial surprise, came together again and the circles closed on him. Abhimanyu was trapped inside.

But fighting the enemy on every side as he advanced, Abhimanyu never looked back. He did not know he had walked into a fatal trap, and if he knew he did not care. Single-handed he fought on, cutting down all who stood against him, using his weapons with such skill and courage that the enemy stood astounded. So he advanced alone, surrounded on all sides by enemies whom he kept at bay. Many he slew as he did the sons of Karna and of Duryodhana, and many great warriors he caused to fly before him, as he did Karna himself. The Kauravas ran in all directions and would have been completely routed if Jayadhratha, king of Sindhus, had not rallied them together and checked their flight. Jayadhratha engaged his attention upon Yudhishthira and the Pandavas, so that they could not advance to help Abhimanyu, while Drona, and five other warriors in chariots surrounded him and gave him battle. But still he fought on. Then Dushahsana cut off his arm with his great sword, but even that did not stop Abhimanyu, for he continued to fight, drenched with the crimson blood that covered his body. Then Dushahsana cut off his limbs one by one.

But Abhimanyu's eyes remained proud and defiant, eager for combat, even while he lay helpless upon the earth. And at this moment Jayadhratha, king of the Sindhus who had fought that whole action without ceasing, returned to the scene. Coming up to Abhimanyu he dealt the final blow that killed him. This deed done, the Kauravas returned to their camp at the sounding of the truce at sunset, rejoicing in the victory they had won.

But for the Pandavas it was a black day. When Abhimanyu did not return, Yudhishthira knew that the worst had happened. His heart grew heavy as he sat waiting; what would he say to Arjuna when that warrior returned? How would he break to him the news of his child's death?

But Arjuna did not need to be told in words. As he and Krishna drove back in the chariot after having defeated the Samsaptakas, Arjuna felt strange forebodings in his heart. In the gathering darkness he seemed to see evil omens: shrouds of death, owls hooting, and corpses and blood. His hands grew cold and his mouth grew dry as, approaching the camp, he heard no joyful sounds of welcome, no music, no laughter. Trembling in every limb, Arjuna entered and

saw his brothers before him, silent, with faces
cast down, and cold fear gripped him. He knew
in his heart, even before Yudhishthira told him.
Then Arjuna sank upon the floor and wept
bitterly. He looked at them standing around him
helplessly and reproached them angrily for
having sent his beloved son to his death. It
was hard, terribly hard for him to bear the
thought that the boy had ventured out alone
and help had not reached him, when he had
most needed it. Bitter were the tears that Arjuna
shed as he cursed himself and his brothers that
night, and no one could console him save his
friend Krishna with his words of deep and
gentle wisdom. All night long Arjuna lay pros-
trate with grief. They brought Subadhra, Abhimanyu's mother, to him and the sweet Uttara,
his bride. Then the sorrowing parents clasped
to them the young girl, and wept over her for
her fate. But Uttara looked at them with strange
calm eyes. "Build me a pyre," she said, "I will
enter the flames and join my beloved Abhimanyu." At that, Arjuna roused himself and
restrained her:

"No!" he cried, holding her. "No, dear one—
this you will not do. You are still young and
you must live." For he knew that she carried

300

in her womb the unborn child of Abhimanyu.
One day the child would grow up and carry
on the name of their clan.

IV

ABHIMANYU AVENGED

The night wore on. The Pandavas sat huddled
in their camp and the only sounds to be heard
were the lamentations of Arjuna. As morning
broke and the first bugle sounded announcing
the beginning of hostilities, Arjuna arose. His
face was grim and set, his fists clenched. He
looked at the weeping women and swore aloud
the terrible oath, that before sunset that day
he would destroy Jayadhratha or would himself
be destroyed. Thus determined, Arjuna mounted
his chariot and leaving Satyaki to defend
Yudhishthira he went to battle.

Now spies had carried to the Kauravas the
news of Arjuna's great oath, and Jayadhratha,
terror-stricken, had wished to fly from the field
of battle. But Duryodhana persuaded him to
remain, promising him that the Kaurava forces
would that day be dedicated solely to the task

of protecting him. Onward sped Arjuna's chariot driven by Krishna, piercing through the Kaurava army, through the lines of their elephants, putting the animals to rout, trampling upon men and causing much panic and confusion. But Arjuna paid no heed to this. Consumed with the single thought of Jayadhratha's destruction he fought his way onward. But as he went on he came face to face with Drona, who barred his way and would not let him go. Arjuna fought hard to overcome him. But Drona proved too strong, and in the end Arjuna had to evade him but only to meet fiercer and more determined opponents at each step, so that it seemed to him for a while, as he fell back fainting and exhausted, that he would be vanquished before his aim could be accomplished. But steeling his heart, he rose up again, panting with the strength of his resolve, and fought his foes and killed them as if they were flies, as he advanced upon his way. And now when he pierced through what seemed to be the very heart of the army, Duryodhana sprang up and faced him, challenging him to a duel. They fought fiercely like a pair of lions and their war cries resounded on all sides. Repeatedly Arjuna attacked Duryodhana, but his shafts

seemed to have lost their power. Then he understood that Duryodhana was protected by a
magic armour that Drona had given him. Desperate was Arjuna and desperately did he fight,
vowing to himself again and again that he would
never give up. Duryodhana meanwhile was
getting exhausted. But already the afternoon was
darkening into evening. Soon the sun would
set; the truce would sound and the fighting
would cease. Once the sun set Duryodhana
knew that he and Jayadhratha were safe.
Arjuna too looked at the western sky, flooded
with the glowing colours of sunset and knew that
the truce was perilously near. Would Arjuna's
great oath remain unfulfilled? Would the death
of Abhimanyu remain unavenged? Would Jayadratha escape his punishment at the hands of
the sorrowing father?

Krishna was watching. He knew that today
Jayadratha must die at the hands of Arjuna.
The sun must not set until Jayadratha had been
killed. As the hour of sunset drew near Krishna
arose and by his power caused the sun to be
shrouded in a mist so heavy that no man could
tell when he set that day. The fighting went on,
for no truce was sounded, the shining arrows
sped like shafts of lightning through the darkness.

Arjuna, who had all but given up hope, saw how he had acquired a fresh lease of time. Gathering new courage and strength he went into the fray once again and, overpowering Duryodhana with arrows carefully aimed at those parts of his body that were not covered with armour, he came at last into the centre of the army formation where Jayadratha hid, full of terror. Then seeing him, Arjuna cried out for vengeance in a terrible voice and let his arrows fly. They went whizzing through the air and slashed Jayadratha's head from his body, and that mighty warrior fell dying to the earth.

Even after this the fighting continued, savage and relentless, far into that terrible night, while the fearful sounds of war shook the earth and the sky. Terrible were the duels that took place between Satyaki and Drona, between Drona and Bhima, Nakula and Karna, between Karna and Bhima; Bhima destroyed seven of Duryodhana's brothers, including even the good and righteous Vikarna, but would himself have been slain by Karna had the latter not remembered his promise to Kunti and spared his life. Last of all came the duel between Karna and the Rakshasa Ghatotkacha, Bhima's son.

In the darkness these two advanced upon each other. Ghatotkacha fought with such great skill and savage fury that Karna surely would have been killed, had he not remembered the mighty weapon which long ago he had acquired from Indra in exchange for his armour and ear-rings. Then in a moment of desperation, forgetting Indra's words of caution, Karna let the thunder-bolt fly. It struck the valiant Ghatotkacha in the chest and he staggered for a moment and then fell, stretched dead upon the ground.

Ghatotkacha was slain. The Pandavas mourned for him and Bhima tore his hair and wept.

Karna had triumphed, but as he turned away from the scene his heart suddenly misgave him. What had he done in his moment of desperation? Had not Indra warned him that the thunderbolt would be useful only once and against but one single enemy? Had he not resolved that he would use it against Arjuna and Arjuna only? Now he had expended that one perfect weapon in a careless, unthinking, desperate moment. He had destroyed Ghototkacha ... but what of Arjuna? Karna turned away. Around him a dark fate seemed to be drawing a web; on all sides its threads seemed to coil themselves around him. Karna's brave heart was heavy with foreboding. But he clenched his teeth; he would fight to the end—to the bitter, tragic end. ..

V

THE DEATH OF DRONA

The slaying of Ghatotkacha did not stop the battle, but only seemed to lash it to new fury as the warriors, their faces dark with anger, their bodies streaming with blood, fought relentlessly on. All night the battle waged and when the pale morning broke, it continued unabated like a never-ending nightmare. It was now the fifteenth day of the war, and it was upon this day that Drona was slain by Dhrishtadyumna. So great had the heat of battle and of men's angry passions become, that the code of the Kshatriyas was again and again thrown aside, and falsehood and treachery were employed in full measure. On both sides men forgot the rules of chivalry and of Kshatriya conduct, and out of one evil action another was born, and another out of that, so that the result was one long chain of evil.

Krishna saw how the battle was going against

the Pandavas. He saw how their forces were scattered like driven rain before Drona's powerful and deadly attacks, and he knew that Drona must die if the Pandavas were to live. But he knew too that once more trickery must come into play, for Drona was too strong for the Pandavas. Krishna leaned over and spoke to Arjuna: "Cry out, Arjuna, cry out aloud that Ashwathama, Drona's son, has been killed! Let the news reach Drona, and when he hears it, he will be so overpowered by sorrow that he will have no more heart to fight. He will sink in dejection, and his hands will lose their grip, his mind its clarity. Thus weakened, Drona might be slain." But Arjuna refused indignantly to stoop to such an unworthy act. Bhima, however, had no such scruples. Knowing that Drona must be destroyed if victory was to be won, he cut down and killed an elephant named Ashwathama, and then he cried out, "Ashwathama is slain!" Now when Drona heard this cry, he was in the midst of battle. He refused to believe it.

"It is not true!" wailed the old man who loved his only son more than his life. "It is a trick they are playing upon me." But Bhima's voice resounded again, "Ashwathama is dead!

Ashwathama, Ashwathama is dead!" Drona turned pale and began to tremble. Yet he could not believe what he had heard. Steadying his fainting heart, he cried out, "I will not believe it until I hear it from Yudhishthira, for Yudhishthira is a man of truth and has never been known to utter a falsehood!" And now Yudhishthira must repeat the lie and cry out that Ashwathama was dead, or be vanquished by Drona, who was already drawing his bow to shoot a deadly and powerful weapon! Hating himself and full of grief and shame, Yudhishthira had now to tell a falsehood, cloaked as a truth. He raised his voice and repeated "Yes, Ashwathama is dead!" and then muttered softly under his breath, "Ashwathama, the elephant!"

At Yudhishthira's words Drona felt the blood drain from his body and the strength ebb from his limbs. His son had been the centre of his life; every action of Drona's had been inspired by love of his son. Now when he heard that Ashwathama had died, Drona's heart failed him. Letting his bow fall, he stood like one dazed upon the battle-field. "What does life hold for me now?" he cried to himself. "What is the use of living now?" Then he sat down where he was, his legs crossed in the lotus posture and

gave himself up to meditation, for now he did
not care for anything, neither the world, nor
victory, nor even his own safety.

As he sat there, weaponless, defenceless, his
mind upon God, there came before him Dhrishtadyumna, the Panchala prince, whose father was
Drona's bitter enemy. He seized Drona by his
white hair and with a mighty cry of revenge,
cut off his venerable head.

At this savage action the warriors around
stood aghast; many men raised their voices
against Dhrishtadyumna's foul deed. Murder
it had been and a grave sin to slay in this manner
a man who was without defence and who was
at prayer. When the truth about the elephant
came to light, they looked with reproachful eyes
at Yudhishthira who had fouled his mouth by
uttering a falsehood. Yudhishthira lowered his
gaze and was silent. He who had been above
untruth had come down to the low level of
ordinary, sinning, lying human creatures. Neither
was it any consolation to Yudhishthira that his
lie had been disguised as a truth. He did not
try to defend himself, for he knew he had acted
wrongly; a lie cloaked as a truth was even more
cowardly and unworthy than a straight and
simple one. He whose life had hitherto been

without the blemish of untruth had now soiled
it. A dark day it was indeed for Yudhishthira,
and he hung his head. Dhrishtadyumna however cared nothing for the qualms that Yudhishthira, Arjuna and Satyaki felt. For he had
achieved the death of Drona and now victory
was almost certain.

Upon Drona's death the Kaurava forces broke
up and fled in wild disorder. But Ashwathama,
the son of Drona, rushed upon the scene and
rallying them, checked the rout. When he heard
of the dastardly manner in which his beloved
father had been done to death, all his anger
came surging up and he put himself into the
fight, determined once and for all to make an
end of Dhrishtadyumna and his friends, the
Pandavas. In his wild fury he released shafts
of explosives and fumes and fires that the
Pandavas had no means of meeting except by
crouching weaponless upon the earth, till they
had sped over them and gone, and the dangers
had passed. This indeed was what they did upon
the advice of Krishna, but the dreadful carnage
continued as the desperate and vengeful Ashwathama rode among them in his chariot like the
very God of Death.

It was only the coming of the night that gave

the Pandavas some respite, for Ashwathama went from the battle-field, exhausted in body and sick at heart, and spent the rest of the hours of that night mourning his father.

VI

KARNA

Upon the death of Drona the Kauravas chose Karna as commander of the army. But the Pandavas' victory was now almost assured. The Kauravas, it seemed, were fighting with their back to the wall. But they did not give up hope, for a true Kshatriya fights to the last and falls bravely upon the battle-field. A Kshatriya will not surrender or fly. And so the Kauravas rallied again under the valiant Karna and went into battle. Neither did they allow their spirits to wane; for they were determined to wrest victory from the very jaws of defeat.

And yet, though they would not acknowledge it, theirs was a rapidly losing battle. The first of their terrible defeats that day came when Bhima defeated Dushahsana and threw him upon the earth. Bhima had lived for this alone, it seemed, to bring about the destruction of the man who had grievously wronged his beloved wife. In a moment of wild animal frenzy Bhima danced on Dushahsana's body and stooped and drank his blood.

One by one the Kauravas had been destroyed, mown down by their cousins whom they had wronged. As the news of his sons' death reached the poor blind king, sitting desolate upon his throne, he wept aloud and wished that he had never been born. Now in this tragic hour he saw how evil, how foolish, his favourite son had been and how his stupidity had carried them all to their ruin. He had allowed him to continue in his wicked ways, and now evil must reap its evil consequences, and fate must proceed relentlessly to take her toll. There was no power on earth that could stop now the dreadful avalanche of wickedness and untruth and murder and death that had been set moving.

This sixteenth day saw what was perhaps the mightiest of combats in the entire war. For it was on this day that Arjuna and Karna came face to face. This time it was indeed the supreme and decisive moment of the war, and it is said that the gods from the heavens came down to watch the battle. The day had opened inauspiciously for Karna. Early, at break of dawn, even as they started out for the scene of action, Shalya, the uncle of Nakula and Sahadeva, king of Madra, he who had been persuaded against his will to fight on the Kaurava side, and who had agreed to be Karna's charioteer, had spoken to him, disparaging his courage and praising Arjuna. Karna, quick-tempered as he was, had quarrelled with him on that account. Thus, even as they started the day, they had fouled its pure air, and clouded their own minds with ugly, angry thoughts.

Shalya took his place in the chariot and drove Karna into battle. As they drove through scenes of bitter fighting on many fronts, Karna's prowess was challenged many times. He fought with each of the Pandava brothers in turn—first with Nakula, from whom he captured his chariot, horses and weapons, so that Nakula had to fly to safety. Karna watched him go, laughing contemptuously. "I would kill you, Nakula, you who run for your life like a rabbit," Karna thought, "but you are too small a prize for me. Besides, there is the promise I made to Kunti!"

Then advancing, proud and defiant, Karna fought Yudhishthira who also took refuge in flight before his terrible onslaught. Bhima pushed

Karna back for a brief while, but the invincible warrior returned with renewed vigour to battle. This second time he defeated the combined attack of the three brothers, Yudhishthira, Nakula and Sahadeva while Bhima held Duryodhana at bay nearby. It seemed at this moment that the battle was turning against the Pandavas, and might be settled once and for all by their defeat. But at that critical moment Arjuna, who had till then been furiously fighting back Ashwathama's attacks, came to the rescue of his brothers, having successfully beaten back the son of Drona.

Now the two mighty warriors, Arjuna and Karna, came at last face to face. They called out to each other with taunts and words of bitter hatred and advanced like storm clouds in the sky. For long they fought, victory alternating between them at each round, while the issue hung doubtful. Karna sent arrows from which came snakes and serpents that hissed terribly and spat out deadly poison. But Arjuna stood his ground, though with difficulty. He sent his answering arrows back with at least as much force and effort as his opponent's.

Then the fatal moment came when Karna's chariot wheel was stuck in the mire. Shalya

informed Karna of this, but would not budge
from the charioteer's seat to help. He had not
forgotten the morning's quarrel, and he sat
sulky and vengeful now, determined to make
things difficult for Karna. Karna cried to Shalya
begging his help, but Shalya shrugged his
shoulders and taunted: "Prove your valour now,
O Karna! Now is the time to show us your much
vaunted skill in war." Karna jumped down.
"Wait, O Arjuna!" he begged. "Stop shooting
your arrows for a while until I free the wheel of
my chariot. You are a man of chivalry and
righteousness and law; surely you will not hit
when your opponent is unable to fight back!"

At this Arjuna was about to lower his bow
when Krishna gave a laugh and spoke to Karna
sharply, reminding him of the many times when
he, Karna, had acted unjustly and unchival-
rously. Karna had sided with the evil Duryodhana and aided him in his wicked ways, said
Krishna. Had he forgotten the day of the
gambling match? Had he forgotten the shaming
of Draupadi? Why had Karna not remembered
the rules of chivalry on that day? Or again,
when the young Abhimanyu had fought alone
and single-handed? Had Karna forgotten? "O
Karna," Krishna called out bitterly, "if you

315

had acted rightly then, things would never have come to this! But having failed, why do you expect others to play fair?" At Krishna's words Karna threw back his head angrily. "Very well!" he said, "I will fight and kill you, even though I do so at a disadvantage." Shalya continued to sit, sulky and unhelpful, in the chariot. From where he stood on the ground, Karna took aim and shot an arrow at his foe, and while Arjuna was engaged in warding it off, he bent quickly and put his shoulder to the wheel. But the wheel had stuck fast in the blood and mire and would not move. Karna left it for a moment and aimed his very best weapons against his foe. So swift and unexpected was this attack that Arjuna staggered back for a moment. The respite he gained thus Karna used to make another attempt to move the chariot wheel. But the web of fate was closing all around him. Luck, fickle, inconstant luck, had deserted him always in his need, and on this last day it was no different. The chariot wheel stuck fast. Karna evaded Arjuna's attacks and lifted his bow to shoot. But as he aimed his arrow Karna felt his hand tremble and his confidence suddenly ebb away. The knowledge of the use of weapons which he had acquired after many years of effort seemed to slip away from him and his mind became a blank. It was the curse of Parashurama having its effect. As his hand shook and slipped, two swift arrows came speeding through the air; one struck the standard of Karna and brought it to the ground while the other cut his head and put an end to the life of this great warrior.

As life left him, it is said that a radiance came from his body, which ascending into heaven, mingled with the light of the sun. Arjuna looked on, dazed by the sight that met his eye and his mind was filled with thoughts that were too deep and sad for words.

Wrong-doing had produced more wrong-doing. Hatred had given birth to hatred. Evil thoughts of revenge had begun a never-ending chain of evil thoughts, and now all round him upon that blood-soaked field were the horrors of a wicked, wicked war, in which the nobler qualities of love, truth, justice, and mercy had been thrown to the winds; only evil flourished and reigned supreme.

No man had escaped from sin. As Arjuna made his way back to the camp he was silent and heavy-hearted. He knew that in all that had happened the Pandavas had been as guilty as the Kauravas.

VII

THE DEFEAT AND DEATH OF DURYODHANA

Long and loud did Duryodhana mourn the death of his friend, weeping inconsolably over his lifeless body, while his few remaining generals stood mutely around him. All, all were gone. Most of his brothers had been slain by the blood-thirsty Bhima. Bhishma had been treacherously cut down and Drona foully murdered. And now Karna! Killed, as they too had been killed, at a moment when he stood defenceless and unarmed! Bitterly did Duryodhana weep, cursing the cruelty of fate.

Then Kripa the teacher spoke, reminding him gently that perhaps he himself was to blame and not fate, for it was he, Duryodhana, who had from the first turned his back upon righteousness, and set events moving because of his jealous, hate-filled thoughts. "You must now cease this terrible war, Duryodhana!" he begged. "Now at least, make your peace with your cousins. Let us not destroy everything." But Duryodhana shook his head. "It is too late now," he said, wearily. "I have come to the point from which there is no return. What hope of peace is left to me now? Better far to fight bravely and die bravely than to give up in the face of difficulty and danger."

Noble were Duryodhana's words, as noble and dignified as they were tragic. Defeat and death he knew were certain, but having come thus far he would not surrender now.

He appointed Shalya commander on the eighteenth day, and they went into battle. But it was a lost game. Yudhishthira met Shalya and after a brave fight killed him, while on another front Sahadeva made short work of Shakuni, the evil genius whose crafty, poisonous mind had been responsible for all that had taken place. And on a third front Bhima took his toll of the surviving brothers of Duryodhana, so that at the end of the day only four warriors remained alive on the Kaurava side—Kripa, Ashwathama, Kirtivarman and Duryodhana.

Then Duryodhana, sick and exhausted, refusing all encouragement, fled at last and took refuge from his enemies among the water weeds, where moor hens and wild ducks nested. And there the Pandavas pursued him, crying out, "Come, Duryodhana, come and do us battle or yield! Why after all these days do you fly like a woman and try to escape death?"

From his shelter Duryodhana answered them wearily, "My friends, my brothers and all whom I held in esteem are dead, killed upon the battle-field. What do I want with an empire now, alone and desolate as I am? Go, Yudhishthira, take my kingdom, take the world and rule it. I give it to you: a kingdom of dead and dying men, and weeping widows and orphaned chil-dren. Take this accursed kingdom and rule it."

But Yudhishthira laughed. "We have come this far," he said. "The struggle is nearly over. I do not need you to make me a gift of what I can easily wrest from you after a fight. Come then and fight us or be forever branded a coward!"

Then Duryodhana reminded them that he was alone against five of them, and Yudhish-thira retorted saying, "You did not think of this, did you, nor your other brave warriors, when Abhimanyu faced you alone and you surrounded him and attacked him on all sides? Still we will show mercy, Duryodhana. Come out from the pond and we will fight you one after another, according to Kshatriya rules.

"I have neither weapons nor armour," Duryo-dhana said. "How can I fight?"

"We will give you both," answered Yudhishthira. "You may choose your weapon and your opponent and fight him."

Duryodhana came out of his hiding place, holding his head high. For his opponent he singled out his enemy and rival, Bhima. For weapon he chose the mace.

Then they fought a mighty duel with their maces, and even then Duryodhana was a formidable opponent for Bhima, aiming his own blows with skill and evading his adversary's with dexterity. It seemed as if the victory that the Pandava had been so sure of winning was slipping from their hands at this last moment, for even Bhima was no match for the desperate Duryodhana.

But as they fought, Krishna made a sign to Bhima, touching his own thigh, and suddenly Bhima remembered the vow he had made that he would break Duryodhana's thighs. He remembered in a flash the assembly hall, the game of dice in which he had been a pawn, and the shame of Draupadi. Anger, red hot anger, filled Bhima, and disregarding the rule of war that the enemy may not be struck below the navel, Bhima lifted up his mighty mace and struck at Duryodhana's thighs and broke them. With a cry of reproach and pain Duryodhana

321

fell bleeding to the ground. Then Bhima in a savage, mad frenzy put his foot upon the fallen man's head and danced triumphantly so that all around stood horror-struck. Yudhishthira rebuked him saying, "Do not trample upon him, Bhima, for Duryodhana is your cousin and a prince. Whatever his faults, whatever our sufferings, your conduct is not worthy of a Kshatriya!"

But Duryodhana, lying upon the ground waiting for his death, laughed at Yudhishthira's words, as his death approached:

"Let him trample upon my head, Yudhishthira. This is not the only unworthy, low act he and you and the other Pandavas have committed. Why, you have won the war, but you cannot deny that you have done so only through unfair means and unrighteous conduct. Bhishma, Drona and Karna were slain in a foul and dishonest manner. Jayadratha by trickery, deceit and cunning was destroyed. And do you think I did not see Krishna making a sign to Bhima, urging him to hit me below the navel upon my thighs? When have you acted in accordance with the Kshatriya code, that you rebuke Bhima now? Let him stamp then upon my crowned head and complete the wheel of wickedness that has been set in motion. His action cannot hurt me. It only hurts him. I am beyond pain or shame. I have been a king and an emperor and have ruled the world and tasted the joy and the power of empire. Kings have bowed before me and done me homage. I have adhered to truth in my own fashion. I have known the loyalty of steadfast friends and of brothers. My life has been full, and now I welcome death as a friend. There is nothing left for me to wish for. For I will go to the warrior's heaven, where dwell those who died bravely in battle. But you, Yudhishthira, you will live and inherit this earth that has been devastated by this war. The curses of the wives you left widowed and mothers you left sonless and children you have orphaned will be upon your head. Go, take your empire. What will it bring you but sorrow and tears?"

Fierce were the emotions that the dying Duryodhana voiced and to the end he remained implacable and unbending. Much of what he said was true, and yet he forgot his own part in the great tragedy. He did not or would not see how it was as much his jealousy and hatred as the Pandavas' wrong-doing, that had been at the root of the evil that had befallen everyone —the death of brave warriors, the crumbling of a mighty empire. Yudhishthira bent his head in shame and grief. He was a man of peace and would not have hurt a fly if he could have helped it. Arjuna's heart wept within him. The Pandavas turned away and left Duryodhana while he writhed in agony. There came to his side Ashwathama and Kirtivarman and the wise Kripa and sat beside him in his final moments.

VIII

ASHWATHAMA

Now the mighty Kurukshetra war was nearly over. But as fire flames up suddenly before it finally dies away, there occurred one more terrible incident that forever closed the tragic chapter.

Ashwathama, bending over the dying Duryodhana, felt his heart sear to see how he had been treacherously done to death. The memory of his father, Drona, came to him too, murdered by Dhrishtadyumna while he was at prayer. And the memory of Bhishma and Karna and all who had fallen. "I will avenge you, O Duryodhana!" Ashwathama whispered fiercely. "I will slay every one of these men!"

Duryodhana smiled and with his dying breath named him commander.

Then upon that dark and sordid night when all lay sleeping, Ashwathama entered the Pandava camp and with his sword cut the throats of every one who slept there—Dhrishtadyumna, his chief enemy, and the five sons of Draupadi and all whom he found, except the five Pandavas and Satyaki and Krishna—these seven who were absent from the camp.

Having done this, he fled from the vengeance he knew would be taken. Nor was he mistaken. For when the news of the slaughter of her sons was brought to Draupadi she cried aloud and swore to kill herself if Ashwathama were not slain. And so the Pandavas pursued him over the wastes of the earth into his secret hiding places and searched and hunted for him. But even now they could not subdue him, for his power was so great that out of a blade of grass he made a weapon of death and sent it against them. When they evaded it, it went like a curse and struck at the womb of Abhimanyu's wife Uttara and at the baby within—so that the Pandavas would have no heirs to succeed them except one, Parikshit.

Having done this, Ashwathama left them,

bitter in heart, a lonely, unhappy soul who wandered alone over the deserted earth for many years till death claimed him at last.

IX

THE END OF THE WAR

Thus ended the war of Kurukshetra, and the bitter rivalry between the sons of the Kuru clan. It was indeed as Duryodhana had cried out, for the blood of the innocent, brave and good men mingled with that of the wicked, the guilty and the low-spirited, and the bodies of the dead lay upon the field in heaps.

There was no Kuru who survived save the blind king and Gandhari and the five Pandavas and their mother. Victory had fallen to the Pandavas, but now that they had the taste of it in their mouths, it was bitter as gall.

All, all had been destroyed in that wicked war, and Yudhishthira felt no joy as he and his brothers made their way slowly to Hastinapura to their uncle, Dhritarashtra.

Broken in spirit and weeping, Dhritarashtra gathered him in his arms. He knew only too well that Yudhishthira had been less to blame in this war than anyone else. Duryodhana had brought it upon himself by his blind stupidity, his unreasoning obstinacy, his jealousy and his hatred. What use blaming anyone now? But as the blind man heard Bhima approach, his anger rose white hot within him. But he smiled sweetly. "Come, Bhima! Come!" he cried, "Let me embrace you." Krishna saw the look of anger and cunning steal into the old man's face as the slayer of his sons stood before him. In an instant he pushed Bhima aside and thrust into the old King's hands a life-size image of iron. Dhritarashtra crushed it in his arms, and so powerful was his embrace that the image shattered into a thousand pieces. Krishna had understood that Bhima would be crushed to death by the king's anger, and had forestalled this and saved the Pandavas.

The brothers came then before the weeping Gandhari, noble and dignified in her grief now as she had always been. They knelt before her, craving her forgiveness humbly, and though her sorrow and anger were so great that they could have scorched the earth, she steadied herself with a wonderful calm and serenity and forgave them the wrongs they had done her.

327

Gandhari reproached only Krishna, knowing that if he had wished it he could have prevented the carnage that had taken place.

"You know all things, Lord," she cried passionately, "yet you remained indifferent while they murdered one another without thought or mercy." Krishna looked at her with compassion. What could he say to this great and noble lady in her grief? What comfort could he give her?

He made no answer at all. In his heart he knew, as she would sooner or later know too, when the first anguish had subsided, that man makes his own fate, and not even the gods can intervene if he is intent upon his destruction.

Then the king and the queen descended the steps of the palace, the Pandavas following, and made their way weeping towards the banks of the river Ganga. As they walked they were joined by hundreds of mourners, widows, and orphans and bereaved old parents. Slowly the sad procession moved through the deserted streets and, arriving at the river, broke into mournful chants of prayer for the souls of the dead. It was then that Kunti revealed at last to her sons that Karna was their brother, for it was they who must perform for him the religious ceremonies that bring peace and tranquility to the souls

of the dead. When Yudhishthira heard this
and as the full meaning of her words dawned
upon him, it seemed to him that the final blow
had been struck and he broke down and wept,
cursing her for having caused him and his
Pandavas to be the enemies and slayers of their
own brother.

"Oh, if you had only spoken," he cried,
"perhaps all this could have been averted!"

But what had happened had happened. The
great tragedy was destined to take place; only
the final scenes now remained to be enacted and
they were being played upon the great stage of
Kurukshetra.

One man was still alive at the end of the war,
and that was the son of Ganga, the valiant
Bhishma, who lay upon his bed of arrows under
the sky, warding off death, for the hour had
not come. Day after day this mighty hero had
lain thus, while the war had raged around him
and arrows, javelins and discuses had sped over
him and past him, and he had seen with compassionate eyes the carnage around him, the
useless anger and killings, the passions and the
heroism of the men who fought.

At the end of the war and after the funeral
ceremonies were over, and after Yudhishthira

329

and the Pandavas had cleansed themselves of
their sins by penance and by bathing in the
waters of the Ganga, it was time for Yudhishthira to be installed as king. Then he with
Krishna went to the field where the vultures
still hovered over the corpses and, coming to
Bhishma, knelt before him to do him homage
and reverence. At Krishna's request Bhishma
spoke to Yudhishthira, instructing him at length
upon his duties as King, upon virtue and upon
life and death and the many, many problems
that man must face during his stay upon the
earth.

Even in his pain, even in death, that brave
fighter bore no ill-will to those who had caused
his fall. Seeing him and hearing him, Yudhishthira knew in his heart that here was the greatest
hero of the day, one of the greatest indeed of all
time. He had lived a long, full life and had
been true to himself and to all around him.
In his youth he had made a great vow and a
great sacrifice, and, having made his promise,
he showed no regret for it; all through his life
he lived in accordance with it. He was a soldier
first and foremost, and his heart did not understand the trickeries and complexities, the wiles
and the cunning of the times. Simple, straight-

forward and plain he spoke in a forthright manner, rebuking where he felt rebuke was deserved, condemning what had to be condemned and praising goodness and virtue and truth wherever he found them. To be good was to him to be himself, taking life as it came and living in simple truth. And because of his utter simplicity and complete honesty he had a wisdom which far surpassed the cunning of smaller men who thought they were clever and shrewd, and well-versed in the ways of the world. Bhishma's was a wisdom so deep and an understanding so clear that he saw ahead as a prophet would do. His was the voice that was raised again and again against the evils of the day— but it was a voice that, alas, went unheeded. Because men would not leave their wickedness, because they would not learn to love instead of hate, to give and share instead of to grasp and grab, there had come about the mighty holocaust in which there was indeed neither victor nor vanquished but only death and destruction.

Every day Krishna led Yudhishthira to the Grandsire where he lay and the old man spoke to him words of wisdom and truth. Day after day he spoke, and while he did so the sun moved steadily northward. Then at last came the day of the winter solstice. Bhishma had wished to see the glory of the sun before he died. When that happened he smiled and called to death to come and take him, and death obeyed his word.

X

Little now remains to be told. Yudhishthira ruled with wisdom and goodness over the domains he had won. As the days passed men began to forget the sorrows of the war, and the wounds in their hearts healed, so that, whatever they may have suffered, they began now to love Yudhishthira and the Pandavas, who worked tirelessly for their good. As for Dhritarashtra and Gandhari who had been bereaved of their hundred sons, Yudhishthira treated them with love and kindness and honour as if they were his own parents and when they died the Pandavas performed their funeral ceremonies.

Yudhishthira and his brothers lived for many years until the time came for them to leave the earth in their turn and travel to the heavenly regions beyond. When that time came the Pandavas were ready. Led by Yudhishthira the four brothers and Draupadi went where death

led them. But before they could enter heaven
one more event took place—one which makes
an oft-told and pleasant story.

It is said that as they went on their way
heavenward Yudhishthira and his brothers found
that they were being followed by their old pet
dog. But when they reached the gates of heaven
the gods, wishing to test them, refused them
entrance. The gate-keeper declared that the
dog was a lowly and unclean animal and so
was barred from entering Heaven's gates. If the
Pandavas wished to enter they must leave the
dog outside. Heaven's joys were not for dogs.
When the Pandavas and Draupadi heard this
they turned away and would not go in, declaring
that they would not forsake the dog that had
served them these many years. They would
rather go to hell, they said, with their dog than
enjoy the good things of heaven without him.
The noble answer so pleased the Gods that they
revealed themselves instantly and opened the
portals of Heaven to the Pandavas and their
wife and their faithful dog. So they entered and
were welcomed by the Gods. And for long they
lived in heaven enjoying the good things of
these regions until at last the time came when
these joys ceased to have meaning. After that

they arose, to that final level of happiness in which man becomes one with the eternal, and is free at last from the cycle of birth and death and re-birth.

The End